70
SEVENTY
EVERYONE NEEDS A TEAM

ENDORSEMENTS

In *Seventy: Everyone Needs a Team*, Dr. Eugene Wilson hits the nail on the head by showing why many churches do not grow and why far too many ministers experience burnout.

Teams are God's answer to the limitations of every leader. Teams are the biblical method of expanding the kingdom of God. Building ministry teams has long been my passion. Dr. Wilson's research, insights, and conclusions will undoubtedly result in more productive team building.

Darrell Johns
Pastor of Atlanta West Pentecostal Church
Atlanta, Georgia

Few books impact me the way *Realign: God-Called Leaders Connecting with Their Purpose* did. And now Eugene Wilson does it again with *Seventy: Everyone Needs a Team*. With tremendous insight on the subject of church leadership and team ministry, Eugene excels.

God is realigning His church with the power of a team to impact our world, and the book you hold in your hand will help you understand how to engage in that journey!

Mark Morgan
Senior Pastor of Abounding Grace
San Francisco, California

One year after releasing his outstanding book *Realign: God-Called Leaders Connecting with Their Purpose*, Eugene Wilson does it again. *Seventy: Everyone Needs a Team* is a must read for everyone who is in leadership or aspiring to lead. It's insightful, biblical, and simple. I couldn't put it down. After reading the last page I found myself wishing there was more.

Bill Hobson
General Secretary of North American Missions
United Pentecostal Church International

I often hear well-meaning Apostolic leaders say, "I want to have an Acts 2 church!" I understand their implied reference to the New Birth message preached by Peter on the Day of Pentecost, and I commend them for their desire to be like the first-century church in *preaching* and in *power*. But there are twenty-seven more chapters in the Book of Acts, and each of them have something to say about the *practice* of the early church. So in reality, I don't just want to be an *Acts 2* church—I want to be a *Book of Acts* church! I've heard my friend Pastor Terry Shock call one of those subsequent chapters "the Acts 6 roadblock." And truly, if the infant church hadn't transitioned from expecting their leaders to do all the ministry into a new paradigm of "team ministry" at that point, much of the revival and harvest that follows in the Book of Acts would have been diminished, or perhaps even forfeited.

In this book, author Eugene Wilson synthesizes biblical and contemporary principles and best practices to give us a bird's eye view of this vital subject. He gives both an honest diagnosis of the issues churches face, and a helpful prognosis for doing ministry *together*. Whether you are a team leader or team member, these perspectives will be helpful to you, and these practices may very well enable you to make an "Acts 6 transition" in your own ministry. And because teams are the *only* biblical way to do ministry, I enthusiastically commend Eugene's writing to you.

Raymond Woodward
Lead Pastor of Capital Community Church
Fredericton, New Brunswick

Eugene Wilson's, *Seventy: Everyone Needs a Team*, addresses one of the divine mandates for the fivefold ministry. While there would appear to be a resistance to any type of apostolic authority in our independent Western culture, we tend to be aware that God has chosen to lead the church through the fivefold ministry (Ephesians 4:11). Tragically, we often ignore one of the primary purposes of this fivefold ministry, ". . . the equipping of the saints for the work of ministry. . . . " (Ephesians 4:12).

Wilson demonstrates how great leaders such as Moses and Jesus recognized that the success of a God-ordained vision hinged on the development of a team, rather than embodying the Lone Ranger mindset that has plagued many leaders. The doctrine of the church being the body of Christ implores contemporary leaders to mobilize His hands and feet in our local congregations in order to realize a God-sized vision. Everyone needs a team.

Brent Coltharp
Lead Pastor of First Apostolic Church
Aurora, Illinois

SEVENTY
EVERYONE NEEDS A TEAM

DR. EUGENE T. WILSON

WORD AFLAME PRESS
HAZELWOOD, MO

**Seventy:
Everyone Needs a Team**
by Eugene T. Wilson

© Copyright 2014 Eugene T. Wilson

Cover Design by Timothy Burk

Published by Word Aflame Press, 8855 Dunn Road, Hazelwood, MO 63042. Printed in the United States of America.

All Scripture quotations in this book are from the New King James Version of the Bible unless otherwise identified.

All rights reserved. No portion of this publication may be reproduced, stored in an electronic system, or transmitted in any form or by any means, electronic, mechanical, photocopy, recording, or otherwise, without the prior permission of Word Aflame Press. Brief quotations may be used in literary reviews.

Library of Congress Cataloging-in-Publication Data
Wilson, Eugene T.
  Seventy : everyone needs a team / by Eugene Wilson.
    pages cm
  Includes bibliographical references and index.
  ISBN 978-0-7577-4622-2 (alk. paper)
 1. Christian leadership. 2. Teams in the workplace. I. Title.
 BV652.1.W51452 2014
 253'.7--dc23
                          2014030892

This book is dedicated to the members of teams who make others shine.

CONTENTS

Preface 11

Acknowledgements 13

A Cry for Help 15

Everyone Needs a Team 29

New Paradigms, Old Purpose 49

Philosophies, Principles, and a King 63

Value-Driven Leadership 79

Building Teams 95

Developing Teams 111

Working with Teams 131

Empowering Teams 153

Epilog 171

Bibliography 173

Endnotes 185

Preface

Jacques Barzun, in *From Dawn to Decadence*, argues that the first step in creating cultural change is the gathering of creative and gifted people. Cultural movement is not the result of a single person who has extraordinary charisma or high intelligence. Rather, cultural movement begins as a clustering of a group of highly creative and gifted people.

Pulitzer Prize winning author Joseph Ellis maintains in *Founding Brothers: The Revolutionary Generation* that the catalytic agent that shaped the new American republic was the personal relationships between George Washington, Alexander Hamilton, Thomas Jefferson, James Madison, and Benjamin Franklin. He states, "Though the American republic became a nation of laws, during the initial phase it also had to be a nation of men."

History shows the revolution was a success because of this cluster of men, not because of one great man. That is not to say that Washington, Hamilton, Jefferson, Madison, and Franklin were not great men. However, the revolution was a collective enterprise that succeeded because of the diversity of personalities and ideologies in the mix. Their interactions and juxtapositions generated a dynamic form of balance and equilibrium, not because any of them was perfect or infallible, but because of their mutual imperfections and fallibilities.

Likewise, the men Jesus assembled to form His team were men of imperfections and fallibilities. Together, however, they helped launch a cultural movement that swept across the entire world.

We live in challenging times. Religion, in general, is not faring well in North America. It is time for a cultural movement to arise. If it should happen, and I believe it will, it will not be the product of an individual. Rather it will be the result of a clustering of a group of people.

This book is about the clustering of a group of people. We call them teams. It is about church leaders recognizing the importance of teams as well as developing and equipping teams. Additionally, it addresses the steps leaders must take and paradigm shifts leaders must make if teams are to function as God intended.

When speaking of teams this book does so in a general sense, and yet at the same time it recognizes that committees, councils, and project groups are not necessarily teams. Groups are not teams just because they consist of more than one person. Likewise, teams consist of more than a group of people. Effective teams share a common purpose and are aligned with it. This is the type of team this book addresses.

I believe the Holy Spirit is leading the church to begin a cultural movement that will shake our world. Will you join with me in this endeavor? Will you consider being a part of a cluster of people that develops teams?

Join with me as we look at Scripture as well as modern day examples in how teams enhance church growth. We will discover that everyone needs a team. Moreover, we will learn how teams transform churches, and transformed churches transform the world.

ACKNOWLEDGEMENTS

Only a fool would think a man could stand alone. Even if no one were with him, he is still not by himself. Others stand beside him even though they are not seen. For you see, a man is a sum of everything he has experienced. He is a product of others, people from yesterday as well as the present. Of this I am certain.

The journey I have traveled and the paths of others that have intersected mine have brought me to where I am today. I am thankful for the journey. I am thankful for those I have met along the way as well as those who have purposefully invested in me. Each one has helped to shape the man I am. Above all, I am thankful for a God who never ceases to amaze me. He guides my every step. Lastly, I am thankful for my wife and children; you bless me. In many ways, this is your book too. You helped to make it what it is. We are a team.

CHAPTER ONE:

A CRY FOR HELP

Take my life!

I Kings 19:4

I was surprised when I heard the news. We were not close, but we were friends. For a few years, we communicated on a weekly basis, mostly through the Internet and occasionally by phone. On a few occasions, while attending some meetings, we were able to spend time together. We connected well; we had something in common—we were both ministers.

The last I heard, he had launched a new church plant targeting generation Y, a generation of whom many are disenfranchised with traditional religion. He had also opened a coffee shop, probably to help offset church expenses as well as to provide a place to connect with people, predominantly those of generation Y.

His methods of ministry were different than mine. He wore dreadlocks and a clergy shirt. Yet in spite of our differences we shared many similarities in our biblical views.

He must have been under enormous pressure. I have experienced it, and you have too. The weight, the stress, trying to fulfill unrealistic expectations—it is not easy. Many quit, just walk away from it. Many have been broken—financially, mentally, emotionally, and spiritually. Sadly, homes have crumbled because of it. And some, like my friend, have committed suicide.

The Problem

What is the problem with church leaders? Why are so many of them under so much pressure? Research suggests a poor understanding of leadership may be a contributing factor. George Barna, in *The Power of Team Leadership*, states,

> We have been taught that leadership is about one individual's performing all of an organization's critical tasks—motivating, mobilizing, directing, and resourcing people to fulfill a vision—at a level of excellence and influence that separates him or her from the bulk of humanity.[1]

The concept of one man being all things to all people is flawed. However, this is generally what people think of when they think of leadership.

People expect extraordinary things of leaders. For example:[2]

- 87 percent expect leaders to motivate people to get involved in meaningful causes and activity.

- 78 percent believe leaders should negotiate compromises and resolve conflicts when they arise.

- 77 percent look to leaders to determine and convey the course of action that people should take in order to produce desirable conditions and outcomes.

- 76 percent rely on leaders to identify and implement courses of action that are in the best interests of society, even if some of those choices are unpopular.

- 75 percent expect leaders to invest their time and energy in training more leaders who will help bring the vision to reality.

- 63 percent want leaders to communicate vision so that they know where things are headed and what it will take to get there.

- 61 percent say leaders are responsible for the direction and production of employees associated with the leader's organization or cause.

- 61 percent think leaders should analyze situations and create the strategies and plans that direct the resources of those who follow them.

- 56 percent hold leaders responsible for managing the day-to-day details of the operation.

These statistics prove it is impossible for any one leader to fulfill all of the expectations of others. "Clearly we have developed an unreasonable notion of what a leader should do."[3]

Upon further reflection, Barna notes the survey shows people hold additional expectations beyond those listed.

> Most people expect the central leader to: direct activity; encourage participants; supply resources; evaluate plans and progress; motivate participants; negotiate agreements; strategize; manage people; reinforce commitments; recruit necessary colleagues; communicate conditions, plans, and assignments; train new leaders; resolve conflicts; and so on.[4]

"Who could possibly meet such a wide range of disparate expectations?"[5] The answer is—absolutely no one.

Unrealistic Expectations

The expectation for pastors is especially high and unrealistic. Dick Iverson, in *Team Ministry*, says,

> The Pastor must be able to know his sheep personally; Instantly available for crisis counseling; Provide assistance during emergencies; Train his people for ministry; Settle interpersonal problems; Maintain discipline; Provide guidance counseling; Admonish and exhort the weary and brokenhearted; Do the work of evangelism; Visit the new "prospects"; Officiate at funerals, weddings, baptisms, dedications; Maintain public relations with the community; Administrate departments efficiently; At times balance the budget; Do janitorial work and maintenance repairs; And, let's not forget

driving the bus. To accomplish all of these feats successfully and always appear to be perfectly calm, relaxed and even tempered would require the combined talents of a superman and wonder woman plus the ambidextrous physical properties of an octopus.[6]

These expectations are absurd and impossible for any one person to fulfill.

To further illustrate the demands people place upon pastors, consider the following:

Researchers have found that pastors are the primary mental health counselors for tens of millions of Americans. They are frequently the first persons to help with a family or marital problem or a personal crisis. The National Institute of Mental Health found that clergy are as likely as mental health specialists to have a person with a *Diagnostic and Statistical Manual of Mental Disorders* diagnosis come to them for help. Clergy are seen for assistance with even the most severe forms of mental illness, including schizophrenia and bi-polar disorder.[7]

While pastors generally want to help people, few are skilled to do so in such extreme cases. Furthermore, few are called by God to do so. Pastors, along with the remaining offices of the fivefold ministry, are called to equip others for the work of ministry. They are not called to meet the expectations of others.

Not Enough Time

Not only do pastors lack some of the skills necessary to meet the expectations of people, they also lack enough time. But this does not stop many pastors from trying. According to research, 80 percent of pastors' wives feel their spouse is overworked.[8] Furthermore, lack of time is one of the most frequently cited work-related stressors amongst pastors.[9]

The results of a survey conducted by Thom Rainer reveal pastors do not have enough time on a weekly basis to meet the expectations of people. Rainer asked twelve deacons in his church to share the minimum amount of time they thought he should average per week in specific areas of congregational responsibilities. He listed twenty areas of responsibility but also allowed the deacons to add other responsibilities, if they saw fit to do so. The following is the minimum expectations the deacons had with regards to pastoral responsibilities and the time that should be spent on each area:[10]

- 14 hours for prayer at the church
- 18 hours for sermon preparation
- 10 hours for outreach and evangelism
- 10 hours for counseling
- 15 hours for hospital and home visits
- 18 hours for administrative functions
- 5 hours for community involvement
- 5 hours for denominational involvement

- 5 hours for church meetings
- 4 hours for worship services/preaching
- 10 hours for a variety of other things

The total amount was 114 hours a week. Rainer says,

> If I met just the minimum expectations of twelve deacons, I would have to work more than 16 hours a day for seven days a week. Or I could take one day off of work each week, and work 19 hours a day for six days a week And remember, I still would only meet the minimum expectations of twelve people in the church, not the entire membership.[11]

Clearly, it is impossible for a church leader to fulfill the unrealistic expectations of others. Steve Schobert, in "Pastoral Ministry: It Takes a Team," states, "It is simply unreasonable to expect that one person, no matter how gifted, can fulfill all the expectations placed on pastors."[12] And yet that is exactly the pressure many church leaders feel on a consistent basis.

Ministerial Pressure Impacts Health

Pressure negatively impacts people's health, especially pastors. Paul Vitello, in an article appearing in the *The New York Times*, states,

> The findings have surfaced with ominous regularity over the last few years, and with little notice: Members of the clergy now suffer from

obesity, hypertension and depression at rates higher than most Americans. In the last decade, their use of antidepressants has risen, while their life expectancy has fallen. Many would change jobs if they could.[13]

Research conducted by Duke University with 1,726 Methodist ministers in North Carolina, over a period of seven years, found that in comparison with their neighbors in their census tracts, ministers experienced significantly higher rates of arthritis, diabetes, high blood pressure, and asthma.[14] The research also revealed that obesity was 10 percent higher among the clergy as opposed to the general public. Likewise, "internal surveys by the Evangelical Lutheran Church in America found that sixty percent of its ministers reported being overweight, sixty percent having high blood pressure, and thirteen percent taking antidepressants."[15]

H. B. London Jr., in *Pastors at Greater Risk*, states that 75 percent of pastors report they've had a significant stress-related crisis at least once in their ministry.[16] And other research shows 70 percent of pastors constantly fight depression.[17]

The poor health of pastors has not gone unnoticed. Numerous denominations have started their own pastor health programs. In 2007 Duke Divinity School began the Duke Clergy Health Initiative, a twelve-million-dollar project initiated to improve the health of United Methodist clergy.[18] And in 2012 the Lilly Foundation committed forty-five million dollars to clergy health and renewal.[19]

While pastors are responsible for eating habits, exercise, and getting adequate rest and relaxation, what are pastors to do about unrealistic expectations? Unrealistic expectations are a major reason why so many pastors are unhealthy. Url Scaramanga, in "Pastors are Fatter, Sicker, & more Depressed," states, "One researcher from Duke University sums it up well: 'These people [clergy] tend to be driven by a sense of a duty to

God to answer every call for help from anybody, and they are virtually called upon all the time, 24/7.'"[20] Clearly, something needs to change.

Ministerial Pressure Impacts Minister's Homes

The pressure of ministry is also felt at home. A recent study conducted by Barna Group reveals pastors named "unrealistic expectation of their kids as the number one reason pastors' kids struggle in the development of their own faith."[21]

H. B. London Jr. shares alarming statistics concerning the negative impact ministry has on pastoral families.[22]

- 80 percent believe that pastoral ministry affects their family negatively.

- 33 percent say that being in ministry is an outright hazard to their family.

- 25 percent of pastors' wives see their husband's work schedule as a source of conflict.

- 80 percent of pastors say they have insufficient time with their spouse.

Furthermore, a survey conducted by Raiford Wheeler with 1,050 participating pastors suggests that ministerial pressure is particularly damaging to pastors' marriages.[23] Seventy-seven percent of the pastors surveyed feel they do not have a good marriage, and 30 percent have had an ongoing affair or had a one-time sexual encounter with a parishioner.

Such statistics, while alarming, give support to the following statistic: among professionals, clergy has the second highest divorce rate[24] with 50 percent of marriages ending in divorce.[25] It is no wonder that the majority of pastor's wives consider the day they entered the ministry to be the most destructive event that has occurred in their marriage, and 80 percent wish their spouse would choose a different profession.[26] The pressure on marriages and homes is tremendous and often devastating. Many do not survive.

Burnout

Merriam-Webster Dictionary defines *burnout* as "exhaustion of physical or emotional strength or motivation usually as a result of prolonged stress or frustration."[27] It has also been described as a combination of three symptoms: emotional exhaustion, increasing depersonalization or cynicism about work, and the feelings of low personal accomplishment.[28] Many church leaders exhibit signs of burnout; many are emotionally exhausted from dealing with people; many have become cynical; and many feel, in spite of their efforts, they are producing little.

The average length of a pastorate is only about four years, and burnout is often the reason why.[29] Research conducted by Barna, Focus on the Family, and Maranatha Life, reveals 80 percent of pastors feel unqualified and discouraged in their role as pastor; 50 percent are so discouraged that they would leave the ministry if they could but have no other way of making a living; and fifteen hundred leave the ministry each month.[30]

The research by Raiford Wheeler, in which he surveyed 1,050 pastors, also revealed[31]

- 100 percent of the pastors had a close associate or seminary buddy who had left the ministry because of burnout, conflict in their church, or from a moral failure.

- 89 percent of the pastors surveyed had considered leaving the ministry at one time.

- 57 percent would leave the ministry if they had a better place to go, including secular work.

- 71 percent of pastors stated they were burned out, and had battled depression beyond fatigue on a weekly and even a daily basis.

Considering such statistics, it is no wonder "sixty percent to eighty percent of those who enter the ministry will have left it ten years later, and only a fraction will stay in it as a lifetime career."[32]

Because of the constant pressure of high expectations, many church leaders consider leaving the ministry. I know of a missionary, who while home on furlough, spoke of being exhausted and needing rest. But at the urging of his superiors, he returned to the mission field. A short time later, the missionary succumbed to temptation. He vainly sought to meet the expectations of others. Unfortunately, it cost him dearly.

I know of a successful minister who once spoke to me concerning his need of a sabbatical. He, however, refused to take one; he was worried what people might think. It wasn't long after our conversation that he experienced moral failure.

I know of an evangelist who sought to meet the demands of a busy calendar, continuing to travel while his wife begged him to stay home. Unfortunately, it cost him his marriage.

I could continue. There are countless stories of other missionaries, other pastors, other evangelists, other ministers and church leaders, who have experienced devastation brought on by burnout.

A few years ago, while visiting the Denali National Park and Preserve in Alaska, I read a quote by National Park Service climbing ranger Daryl Miller. He said,

> The chance for something to go wrong is highest on a summit push. People sometimes underestimate how hard it is to come back from the summit. They use most of their energy to go to the top, and when they are descending, balance and strength are gone. Eighty-five percent of all accidents on Denali happen during the descent, usually after a summit push.

Similarly, many church leaders extend great energy trying to get to the top, in expanding ministries, growing churches, having revival, and so on. Unfortunately, some never complete the journey. Richard Krejcir, in "Statistics on Pastors," notes that over 90 percent of those who enter the ministry start off right, but then something derails them.[33] That something is often associated with trying to meet unrealistic expectations.

Moses and Elijah

Scripture reveals that Moses and Elijah had several things in common. Both men built an altar made of twelve stones. Both men stood fearlessly before powerful and evil rulers. Both men worked miracles. Both men fasted for forty days. Both men had extraordinary experiences on the top of a mountain. And both men appeared together on the Mount of Transfiguration. Additionally, both men, because of enormous pressure, asked God to take their lives. Moses said, "If You treat me like this, please kill me here and now—if I have found favor in Your sight—and do not let me see my wretchedness!"[34] And Elijah said, "It is enough! Now, LORD, take my life, for I am no better than my fathers!"[35]

Both men displayed classic symptoms of burnout: emotional exhaustion, increased depersonalization or cynicism of ministry, and low personal accomplishment. Moses struggled meeting the high expectations of the people, while Elijah experienced physical and emotional exhaustion after having killed four hundred and fifty false prophets of Baal.

Perhaps Moses thought the display of God's power in Israel's deliverance from Egypt, crossing of the Red Sea waters, and miraculous provisions would remove all doubt from Israel. If so, he was mistaken. And perhaps Elijah thought fire falling from heaven would result in the conversion of the nation. If so, he too was mistaken. Consequently, it may have been unfulfilled expectations that caused Moses and Elijah to bottom out.

Is it possible that the most damaging expectations are of our own making? Are we most discouraged when our own expectations are unfulfilled? It is unrealistic to think we can fulfill the expectations of others; why then do we think our own expectations will be fulfilled? High expectations, whether it is the expectations of others or of our own doing, are having a negative impact on our lives. We cannot afford to continue trying to meet them. Something must give.

Conclusion

It seems ironic that we would idolize Moses and Elijah, both of whom asked to die, and look down on others who, like my friend, commit suicide. Before we criticize those who have checked out, we should take a long look in the mirror. Some of us have checked out too. Some of us let our dreams die somewhere back in time. And some of us, like Elijah, who felt he was alone in his zeal for God, feel we are alone. But he was not alone. There were seven thousand others who also refused to bow down. Neither are we alone, in spite of how we may feel.

Mercifully, God did not answer the prayers of Moses and Elijah and take their lives. He had something better in mind. God took some of the Spirit that was upon Moses and put it on seventy others. And God ordered Elijah to anoint Elisha. God's answer to prayers prayed in frustration was to instruct Moses and Elijah to build teams. Thankfully, God does not answer some of our prayers the way we pray them. Instead, He has something better in mind.

CHAPTER TWO:

EVERYONE NEEDS A TEAM

. . . about eight day's after. . . .

Luke 9:28

It is unusual to think of Moses and Elijah within the same context. It is more common to think of Moses and Joshua together, or Elijah and Elisha, not Moses and Elijah. They lived some five hundred years apart. Moses lived some fourteen hundred years before Christ; Elijah lived some nine hundred years before Christ. Yet despite the years that separated the two prophets, the Synoptic Gospels—Matthew, Mark, and Luke—have them together at the Mount of Transfiguration.

What is the significance of Moses and Elijah with Christ at the Mount of Transfiguration? Why wasn't Abraham, the father of the faithful, at the Mount of Transfiguration? And David, a man after God's own heart? Furthermore, what is the significance of the phrase, "about eight days after"? Does it offer us any insight as to why Moses and Elijah appeared on the Mount?

Luke 9:28 says, "Now it came to pass, about eight days after these sayings, that He took Peter, John, and James and went up on the mountain to pray." Luke's mention of "about eight days after" links two events together—what occurred at the Mount of Transfiguration with what occurred eight days prior to the Mount of Transfiguration.

About eight days prior to the Mount of Transfiguration, we find Jesus talking with His disciples and asking them,

> "Who do men say that I am?" So they answered, "John the Baptist; but some say, Elijah; and others, one of the prophets." He said to them, "But who do you say that I am?" Peter answered and said to Him, "You are the Christ."[36]

Upon Peter's confession, Jesus responded that flesh and blood had not revealed this unto Peter, the Father had. Jesus then began to speak of His impending death, that He would suffer many things and be rejected by men.

Peter, not liking what he was hearing, took Jesus "aside and began to rebuke Him" (Mark 8:32). Mark notes that Jesus, in turn, rebuked Peter, saying, "Get behind Me, Satan! For you are not mindful of the things of God, but the things of men" (Mark 8:33).

Peter was eager to have a King with a crown but averse to having a King with a cross. A crown meant Peter would have a place of distinction and prominence in the Kingdom. A crown meant Peter would be vindicated for having left it all. Peter would be something more than a lowly fisherman. But a cross? What future was there to be had in a cross?

Jesus continues,

> Then He said to them all, "If anyone desires to come after Me, let him deny himself, and take up his cross daily, and follow Me. For whoever

desires to save his life will lose it, but whoever loses his life for My sake will save it."[37]

Jesus, in essence, tells Peter, along with the other disciples, not only am I going the way of the cross, you will too, that is, if you decide to follow me.

About eight days later, Jesus takes Peter, James, and John with Him to the mountain and Moses and Elijah appear. What was the subject of conversation? Luke 9:31 remarks that they talked about "His decease which He was about to accomplish at Jerusalem." The subject matter was the same as eight days prior—Christ's impending death.

So what is the significance of Moses and Elijah with Christ on the Mount of Transfiguration? It is found in the subject matter—death and what would result from it, ministerial expansion. Death and the result of death, or ministerial expansion, is the one common denominator in all three men.

Upon Moses praying, "God let me die," the Lord said to Moses,

> Gather to Me seventy men of the elders of Israel, whom you know to be the elders of the people and officers over them; bring them to the tabernacle of meeting, that they may stand there with you. Then I will come down and talk with you there. I will take of the Spirit that is upon you and will put the same upon them; and they shall bear the burden of the people with you, that you may not bear it yourself alone.[38]

Likewise, when Elijah prayed for death the Lord instructed him to anoint Elisha.[39] The purpose of Moses and Elijah's appearance on the Mount of Transfiguration was to prove that the death of Jesus Christ would not be the end. Instead, it would result in the expansion of a ministerial team; the entire world would soon hear the gospel message.

It was expedient for Jesus to leave; the Holy Spirit was coming.[40] Many would be empowered. More would be accomplished through the efforts of a team than Christ could ever accomplish alone. The future was not dependent upon one gifted leader. It was dependent upon the development and empowerment of others.

Team Defined

What is the essence of a team? The term *team* has been defined as "a group of people who work together."[41] It has also been described as "a group of people with a full set of complementary skills required to complete a task, job, or project."[42] Jon Katzenbach and Douglas Smith, in *The Wisdom of Teams*, define team as "a small number of people with complementary skills who are committed to a common purpose, performance goals, and approach for which they are mutually accountable."[43] Hence, a team is a group of people working together for a common purpose or goal.

The definition of team is closely associated with the definition of leadership. Peter Northcuse, in *Leadership: Theory and Practice*, defines leadership as "a process whereby an individual influences a group of individuals to achieve a common goal."[44] Henry and Richard Blackaby, in *Spiritual Leadership*, define spiritual leadership as leading people away from self-centered plans and purposes to fulfilling God's plans and purposes.[45]

Hence, teams, within the context of the church, involve leaders and followers orbiting around Christ-centered principles, purposes, and goals, void of selfish ambition or self-centered pursuits. Moreover, the purpose of teams is not found in fulfilling the vision, purpose, or mission of leaders. The purpose of teams is found in achieving mutual goals, goals that leaders and followers are committed to and hold one another mutually accountable for.

Scriptural Support

The Bible supports the concept of ministerial teams. The "Great Man theory," which offers a possible model for leadership, believes history can be explained by the impact of "great men." Such great men are thought to have great charisma, intelligence, or wisdom.[46] The theory endorses the thought that a man is either born great or not so great. A careful rendering of Scripture, however, reveals the "Great Man theory" is inaccurate. Ministry is seldom, if ever, about one extraordinary man.

The idea that leadership is a team concept rather than an individual concept is challenging to many. United States is the most individualistic nation in the world.[47] Consequently, we are more likely to view Scripture through the lens of individuality rather than a collective body. We are more likely to see support for the "Great Man theory" than we are for teams. Notice, however, the following examples of teams in Scripture:

Moses

Although Moses was chosen by God to lead the children of Israel, he was unable to lead alone. Others were needed. On more than one instance Moses staggered under the weight of leadership. When the first instance occurred, Jethro, Moses' father-in-law, having observed Moses working with an unsustainable model of leadership, offered corrective counsel. His counsel centered on the building of a team. Jethro suggested Moses appoint able men over tens, fifties, hundreds, and thousands to help as judges of the people. The second instance "came through the direct intervention of God, who provided seventy elders to help bear the burden of the people with Moses."[48] In both instances, Moses "found relief in sharing authority with others."[49]

Jesus

Jesus not only worked with a specific team, He had multiple teams. He had a team of twelve, the disciples; and a smaller team of three, Peter, James, and John. He also had a team of seventy. Moreover, He sent out missionary teams in groups of two. He did this with the twelve as well as the seventy.

Paul

Paul offers another example of teams at work in Scripture. Paul's ministry mostly took place within the context of teams. Paul began his ministry as an associate of Barnabas. He then branched out on his own, but not without a team. We find Paul working closely with Silas, John Mark, Timothy, Luke, Priscilla and Aquila, Titus, and Erasmus. There are seven others who are mentioned by name as ministry partners, and many others who are listed at the conclusion of his letters.

Metaphors

Scriptural support for teams can be found in metaphors used in Scripture to describe the church. Each metaphor helps us appreciate the church more, what its purpose is, and how it functions. One of the spiritual metaphors used for the church is family. Wayne Grudem, in *Systematic Theology*, states,

> The fact that the church is like a family should increase our love and fellowship with one another. The thought that the church is like the bride of Christ should stimulate us to strive for greater purity and holiness, and also greater love for

Christ and submission to him. The image of the church as branches in a vine should cause us to rest in him more fully. The idea of an agricultural crop should encourage us to continue growing in the Christian life and obtaining for ourselves and others the proper spiritual nutrients to grow. The picture of the church as God's new temple should increase our awareness of God's very presence dwelling in our midst as we meet. The concept of the church as a priesthood should help us to see more clearly the delight God has in the sacrifices of praise and good deeds that we offer to him (see Hebrews 13:15-16). The metaphor of the church as the body of Christ should increase our interdependence on one another and our appreciation of the diversity of gifts within the body.[50]

The church is a body. Paul taught the importance of all of the members of the body functioning as God intended. Why? Because "all of us can do more than one of us."[51]

Teams Generate Synergy

One of my favorite biblical stories is when Jonathan took his armor bearer with him, climbed a cliff, and engaged in a fight with about twenty Philistines. There were only two swords in the entire Israelite camp—King Saul had one, Jonathan the other. The Israelite army was at a great disadvantage. But Jonathan says to his armor bearer, "Perhaps the LORD will help us, for nothing can hinder the LORD. He can win a battle whether he has many warriors or only a few!" (I Samuel 14:6, NLT). The following describes what happens next and is garnered from verses 13-22:

So they climbed up using both hands and feet, and the Philistines fell before Jonathan, and his armor bearer killed those who came behind them. They killed some twenty men in all.

Suddenly, panic broke out in the Philistine army, both in the camp and in the field, including even the outposts and raiding parties.

Then Saul and all his men rushed out to the battle and found the Philistines killing each other.

Even the Hebrews who had previously gone over to the Philistine army revolted and joined in with Saul, Jonathan, and the rest of the Israelites. Likewise, the men of Israel who were hiding in the hill country of Ephraim joined the chase when they saw the Philistines running away.

This story is a powerful example of synergy. Synergy is defined as "the increased effectiveness that results when two or more people (or groups) work together."[52] Synergy means a team can outperform the effort of the best member of the team. Synergy also means a team will produce a better result than if each person within the group was working toward the same goal as individual members.[53]

Pat Croce, in *I Feel Great and You Will Too,* shares the following:[54]

A motorist was driving down a lonely road when he blew a tire, skidded into a ditch and flipped his car upside down. He managed to get out of the car but knew that he was in the middle of nowhere.

About the time he was ready to panic, a farmer came down the road in a cart pulled by a blind mule named Gus. The farmer offered to have Gus pull the car out of the ditch.

The man was very skeptical because Gus the blind mule looked very weak and frail but he agreed anyway as he had no other options to get his car back on the road.

The farmer hitched Gus the blind mule to the car, cracked his whip in the air and yelled…

> "Yaaa there Sam! Pull! Pull!"
>
> The mule did not move.
>
> The farmer cracked his whip again and yelled out,
>
> "Yaaa there Jake! Pull! Pull!"
>
> The mule did not move.
>
> Once more the farmer cracked his whip and shouted,
>
> "Yaaa there Pete! Pull! Pull!"
>
> Still Gus did not move.

And then the farmer cracked his whip and shouted,

"Yaaa there Gus! Pull! Pull!"

And at that moment, Gus dug in his scrawny hind legs, pushed through the dirt, and surged forward.

Soon enough the car turned right side up and came rolling out of the ditch and back onto the road. The motorist was shocked, appreciative, and curious. He asked the farmer why he called out all those other names.

The farmer simply replied that Gus is blind and if he thought it was just up to him alone to pull that car out of the ditch, he wouldn't have even tried. But, when he thought he had the help and support of others, he was much stronger than he even knew he could be.

Many people seem to recognize the value of teams, and yet many people function in ways that are detrimental to teams. Croce continues, "We've all got some blind mule in us. If we are lucky, we've got some of that farmer in us, too."[55]

Teams Enhance Church Expansion

When people work together the possibility of success is enhanced; this includes church expansion. Acts 6:1-7 is an example of how teams can heighten the possibility of church growth. Acts 6:1 (NIV) states, "in those days . . . the number of disciples was increasing." Acts 6:7 (NIV) records, "the number of disciples in Jerusalem increased rapidly." In between these two statements, however, exists a situation that could have derailed the expansion of the church.

What was the issue? The Hellenistic Jews were complaining against the Hebraic Jews because their widows were being overlooked in the daily distribution of food. The root of the problem was language differences between the two groups. Phillip W. Sell, in "The Seven in Acts 6 as a Ministry Team," explains:

> The Hebraic Jews were natives of Palestine who spoke a Semitic language, probably Aramaic. The apostles were no doubt identified with these Hebrews. The Grecian Jews were Jews of the Diaspora who spoke Greek and had been raised in Hellenistic culture.[56]

Differences in language had produced both Aramaic- and Greek-speaking synagogues, and these pre-existing tensions were manifesting themselves within the church.[57] "Greek-speaking Jews, sensitive to presumptions of superiority on the part of the Aramaic speaking Jews," viewed the failure to take care of its widows "to be a ground for second-class treatment."[58]

Interestingly, no accusation is directed towards the apostles, as though the apostles had done wrong, and no mention is made of a breakdown in the system for distributing goods, only that "their widows were neglected in the daily distribution" (Acts 6:1). The problem was much deeper than food distribution; the problem was the "Grecian Jews' perception of prejudice treatment."[59]

Remarkably, the apostles did not correct or discipline the Hellenistic Jews for being divisive; nor did they instruct the church on the importance of unity. Instead, the apostles instructed the church to select seven men of "good reputation, full of the Holy Spirit and wisdom" (Acts 6:3) to oversee the distribution of goods.

Why were such high standards needed for the distribution of food? The answer is, the issue at hand consisted of more than a simple breakdown in the distribution of goods. The root of the problem was the perceived prejudice and unfair treatment of the Hellenistic Jews. Wisdom would be needed to deal with the root problem. The seven men would need to function under the influence of the Holy Spirit in dealing with the source of the problem.

Philip W. Sell makes an interesting observation:

> Of interest is the fact that all of the names are Greek, not Hebrew, and one of the seven, Nicolas of Antioch, was not Jewish by birth but was a proselyte. Probably they were all Greek-speaking. They were no doubt sensitive to the needs of the Grecian Jews.[60]

The root issue was addressed when the people were empowered to choose seven men.

Luke records the end result. Many priests became believers. Individuals, who by virtue of their work had witnessed the hypocrisy of Jewish leaders, were moved by the actions of the apostles who not only proclaimed the Word but also lived the Word. Because of the apostles' response to the situation, because a team was built, church expansion occurred.

The growth of the church was not dependent on the apostles cramming more into their already busy schedule. The solution to the problem at hand was not the use of power and authority in demanding the people to be unified. The solution was centered on the building and empowering of a team of seven.

The apostles' handling of the Acts 6 crisis should be considered as a viable alternative to the way many church leaders deal with issues. Church leaders are often guilty of labeling problems as evil spirits. Furthermore, many church leaders are guilty of trying to handle problems by themselves. Rather than extend trust during times of crises, church leaders usually trust people less. During times of crises few church leaders would consider ministerial expansion or the building of a team as a priority. And during times of crises few church leaders willingly engage in self-evaluation. Instead, it is more common to blame others. The apostles, however, did things differently than most church leaders, and as a result, the church grew.

Breakout Churches

What does it take for a church to break out of mediocrity? This was the question posed by Thom Rainer and his research team in a landmark study of churches in North America. Rainer shares the results of the research in his book, *Breakout Churches*.[61] For the purposes of the research, a breakout church was defined as a congregation that had experienced at least five years of decline before experiencing at least five years of expansion. Although a common factor in breakout churches is often a change of pastors, for the purposes of the study, the research looked at churches that had experienced a breakout without changing pastors. Thirteen churches met the criteria.

Interestingly, almost without an exception, the research discovered seven common characteristics:[62]

>   1. The pastor had a "wake-up" call. He stopped denying that his church had a challenge. He became determined, in God's power, to lead the church to

greater health. He would no longer be satisfied with mediocrity in God's church.

2. The church, under the pastor's new leadership, developed clarity in its purpose. Most of the churches were previously activity focused. They were busy with the "what" without addressing the "why."

3. The pastor began assembling the right team for a new era of leadership. That team would include either paid staff or unpaid laypersons.

4. The pastor developed a spirit of tenacity. He knew that the turnaround would not take place overnight. He followed a prayerful plan for the long haul.

5. One of the early moves in these churches was to focus more ministries outwardly. The wake-up call noted above included an awareness that most of the ministries of the church were for the comfort and desires of the members. The leaders began to change that reality.

6. The pastor and other leaders in the breakout churches had deep biblical faithfulness. They saw their mission emanating from God and written in His Word. That faithfulness was the push that moved them forward even in the

midst of challenging times and potential discouragement.

7. The pastor invested more time in the preaching ministry. He realized the centrality of the preached Word, and gave it more time and emphasis than at any point previously.

The importance of teams in breakout churches is apparent. Not only do pastors of breakout churches assemble the right team, they develop and empower the team. Teams are essential in breakout churches. It is impossible for one man to turn a church around without the support of others. Teams are needed.

Why Some Churches Are Declining

According to the National Congregations Study, 11 percent of people attending worship services attend small churches.[63] The study also reveals the future of one-third of the churches in the United States, which are small churches, is being seriously threatened, largely due to a declining membership and financial base.[64]

Meanwhile, 50 percent of churchgoers attend the largest 10 percent of churches in America, that is, churches with an average attendance of 350 or more.[65] And 83 percent of evangelical churches with more than 1,000 people are increasing in church attendance.[66]

What is a telling difference between large churches and small churches, beyond differences in size of buildings and budgets? Why are large churches growing larger, while many small churches are growing smaller? Could the answer be teams? Many small churches do not have teams, or have very few of them. Nor do they see the value in them. Large churches, however, cannot exist without them.

Not everyone who attends a large church is active in a ministry. However, it is wrong to assume that the motive for people who attend large churches is to escape involvement in ministry. People want to be a part of something meaningful. The reason large churches are often more attractive than small churches is because large churches offer ample opportunity for people to serve on a team. Opportunities for involvement in small churches commonly do not involve a team. If a person is to succeed in ministry in a small church, it usually involves doing ministry alone.

One of the reasons teams thrive in large churches is because large churches promote the team concept. Large churches tend to have a well-defined path, structure, and system for growing people. In large churches, people are encouraged, on a regular basis, to get involved in ministry, and many opportunities exist for involvement. In contrast, although most small churches need help, opportunities for meaningful involvement are usually limited to a few areas. Yet another difference between small churches and large churches is that large churches routinely help people discover their ministry, gifting, and calling. In small churches, people are usually left to figure this out on their own.

The Pastor-Centric Model Stunts Church Growth

If the church is going to be what God wants the church to be, churches, as well as church leaders, must rid themselves of the pastor-centric mindset. Everything does not revolve around the pastor. Pastors are not called to do the bulk of the work of ministry, while everyone else is the beneficiary.[67]

The word *pastor* means shepherd; a pastor is a tender or keeper of the flock.[68] Unfortunately, many interpret this to mean pastors are to do the work of ministry. According to

Ephesians 4:11-12, however, this thinking is not accurate. Pastors are not called to do the work of ministry; pastors are called to equip others for their work of ministry.

Alan Nelson, in an article titled "From Me to We," states,

> After more than 20 years as a pastor, two church plants, and serving in both small and large venues, I've come to believe that the sing e biggest barrier to churches reaching their potential is this: the pastor-centric model of ministry.[69]

We must rid ourselves of the pastor-centric mindset. The focus of Ephesians 4:11-12 is the purpose of the fivefold ministry—the equipping of the saints for the work of ministry. The focus is not a particular function or gifting, or authority, or hierarch, and so on. The focus of Ephesians 4:11-12 is about a plurality of leaders whose responsibility is to equip others for their work of ministry. Ephesians 4:11-12 is about teams. Teams enhance growth. Teams generate synergy. Teams equip people.

Church leaders need to grow in leadership ability and ministerial ability. But church leaders must not be given to self-centeredness by seeking self-improvement. Paul addresses this issue in Philippians 2:4, "Let each of you look out not only for his own interests, but also for the interests of others."

Many of the voices on the subject of leadership presume a "high-profile, multitalented, popular icon in the center-stage spotlight."[70] The majority of leadership books "discuss the indispensable skills needed to become king of the hill; [while] few downplay personal superiority or emphasize serving within a team context."[71] Unfortunately, the culture of leadership within the church is much like the world's.

Why do some church leaders act in ways detrimental in the developing and empowering of teams? One of the reasons is because some leaders do not like uncertainty. They are afraid of losing control. But we are not called to control. In fact, Jesus taught against such leadership.

Church leaders who control things use the metaphor of a shepherd as the basis for doing so. That is, some view their calling as a shepherd as a God-given right to control people. But this is a gross misrepresentation of what Scripture advocates when it comes to leadership. They forget they are not "the shepherd"; they are "under shepherds." Additionally, some church leaders fail to understand that a shepherd is a metaphor, not an actuality, and with any metaphor there are limitations.

Church leaders who think they have a biblical right to command and control people are in direct violation of scriptural principle. Church leaders are called to equip, not control. People cannot fully function in their God-called ministries when church leaders control the entire ministry. When church leaders control the ministry of the people, church growth is stunted.

Another problem with pastor-centric leaders is that they deplete themselves of energy. God's plan for the ministry never included ministry burnout. Steve Schobert states,

> The burden and responsibility of pastoral care was never meant to be carried alone. The pastoral task is larger than any one person's abilities, gifts, or energy resources. It takes a team of gifted and called leaders to respond to the immense task of pastoral leadership. Abandoning the unrealistic expectations commonly placed on pastors and adopting a biblical model of team ministry leadership offers the best hope for the health and sustainability of pastors and the churches that they serve.[72]

The solution to burnout is for church leaders to allow others to share the load.

Why Are There Not More Breakout Churches?

Why was the Rainer research team only able to identify thirteen breakout churches? Why not more? Rainer suggests four possibilities:[73]

1. Lack of leadership development. Most pastors have little training or background in leadership. But they are expected to lead a church. Some may have extensive theological and biblical training, but they are weak in leadership. Jethro had to tell Moses that his leadership approach was all wrong. Moses was headed for a leadership disaster. Many of our churches have leaders who have few leadership skills.

2. Unbiblical understanding of church membership. Basically, an unbiblical understanding of church membership is one that is self-centered. Members have an attitude that the church exists for "me" and "my" preferences. If I don't get my way, I'm either going to cause conflict or leave the church.

3. Unclear purpose. Though it may seem counterintuitive, many church members do not know the clear purpose or purposes of their church. The purpose is the guiding statement that points

members to all that they should do in the church. Without a clear and biblical purpose, members either fail to make meaningful contributions or they exit the church.

4. Lack of outward focus. In the American church, over 95 percent of all money and time resources go toward the members instead of those outside the church. Until a church gains a clear outward mindset, it will have little opportunity to be a true breakout church.

The reason why there are not more breakout churches largely revolves around the lack of teams, systems, and structures necessary for teams to thrive. Which makes one wonder, *If teams were a vital aspect of churches, would there be any need to breakout?* Is there the possibility that teams, functioning the way God intended for them to function, are the answer to sustainable growth? It certainly seems so.

Conclusion

Stagnant churches cannot continue to do the same thing they have been doing and expect different results than what they have been getting. Therefore, in order for stagnant churches to experience a turnaround, change is necessary. What does this change consist of? Where does the change begin? It begins with church leaders, and it consists of church leaders building, developing, and empowering teams. But for this to happen church leaders must first examine the philosophies by which they function.

CHAPTER THREE:

NEW PARADIGMS, OLD PURPOSE

> . . . the eyes of your understanding being enlightened. . . .
>
> Ephesians 1:18

Church leaders need to experience a paradigm shift. They need to see things the way God sees them, especially with regard to leadership. Aubrey Malphurs and Will Mancini, in *Building Leaders*, maintains,

> We need a radical change in the typical twenty-first-century pastor's church-leadership paradigm, especially if the pastor attended a classical seminary or is an older person. Pastoral ministry certainly includes the central responsibilities of teaching and preaching the Bible, but far too many pastors stop there. Leading a church in today's and tomorrow's world involves training leaders who will develop other leaders to carry the ministry torch to the third and fourth generations. The danger is that some denominational executives and pastors

will continue to believe that a single initiative program, such as preaching the Bible or pastoral care, accomplishes the ministry.[74]

Church leaders have often looked to programs as the answer to church growth. Thus, when church leaders speak of changing things it usually involves changing from one program to another. But programs are neither the problem nor the solution. We must dig deeper if we want to experience change that makes a difference.

The change that is needed is a change of mindset, and a change of mindset is one of the most difficult changes to make. It is much easier to change a program than to change the way we think. Changing the way we think involves seeing the reality. Most of us, however, struggle with seeing the reality, and our inability to see it is the reason why most of our change initiatives fail.

Questions

Seeing reality involves our seeing things as they are. Not as we hope or think things might be. This is why asking the right questions is so crucial. Asking the right questions helps us to discover the reality. By asking the right questions we can identify the problem and generate the correct solution. Our solutions are invalid if we failed to identify accurately the root problem. If we do not identify the root problem, by asking the right questions, we may end up changing things that don't need changing. This is so simple but often overlooked by many church leaders.

Questions help detect errors. Jesus was a master at asking the right question. The Synoptic authors record that Jesus asked one hundred and eighty-seven questions in response to being asked a question. Jesus asked questions and helped others see how their thinking was flawed. Our use of questions can be beneficial in helping us dig deep.

It is impossible to solve a problem that has not been defined. Solutions to poorly defined problems end up being poor solutions. Unfortunately, this happens all too often. For example, I have heard many sermons preached on the subject of prayer, with special emphasis placed on *you ought to*. Unfortunately, I have heard little instruction on how to pray. Furthermore, I have seen even fewer who lived a life of prayer.

I offer the above as an example. The point is if we misdiagnose the problem, we will administer the wrong solution. Often times the problem is not unwillingness on the part of people to do what needs to be done; the problem is often a lack of knowledge or know how. And yet many continue to major on *ought to* rather than *how to.*

I once taught a series of lessons on man's need to apply the Word of God to his life. I spoke concerning the difference between the wise man and the foolish man—the wise man heard the Word and applied it; the foolish man heard the Word but did not apply it.

During this time I met with a young couple for marriage counseling. The husband had recently confessed to an affair, and subsequently, lost his job. As I spoke with them concerning the importance of applying God's Word, I felt a strong impression from the Holy Spirit—they don't know how. So I asked the couple to describe to me ways in which they could apply the Word of God to their present situation. They stared at me with blank expressions. Over the course of the next few weeks I helped lead the couple in applying God's Word to their lives. I will never forget the husband walking into my office with a notebook filled with Scriptures and insights God was revealing to him. Thankfully, the couple applied those insights and their marriage was restored.

This couple is not unusual; many people need less *ought to* and more *how to* sermons. Again, I offer this as an example of the importance in asking the right questions. The importance of asking the right questions cannot be understated. If we continue to ask the wrong questions we will continue to generate the wrong solutions.

Questions with Regard to Teams

This book is about the need for teams; it is about developing, equipping, and empowering teams. Based on personal observation, one of the first things that must be addressed is our mindset as to why people are not actively engaged in ministry.

We think people don't want to be involved. We think people don't care. We think people don't want to commit. We think people lack submission. We think people don't respect authority. And because we think these things are spiritual issues, we preach about the need for people to care. We preach commitment. We preach submission. We preach respect for spiritual authority. But is the problem really a lack of submission? Or a lack of respect? Or a lack of commitment?

The issue is not what we think it is. The reason why people are noncommittal with regard to ministry is that we are not asking the right questions. Alas, we have yet to accurately identify the root problem. So what questions should we ask?

We should ask questions such as:

- What is our mission?

- What is our purpose?

- What is our vision?

- What are our values?

- What behaviors, attitudes, or beliefs are interfering with our mission, purpose, vision, and values?

- What is a win?

- How do we measure success and is it a biblically-sound measurement?

Such questions help us identify the heart of the matter.

Why aren't more people involved in ministry? Why aren't more people committed? Why are not teams flourishing within the church? Could part of the problem be our failure, as church leaders, to align with our purpose?

Many church leaders have flawed philosophies about ministry. On what do I base my charge? I base it on the fact that few of us would have responded the way the apostles did in Acts 6. Most of us, given the same circumstances, would not have expanded the ministerial team. Instead, most of us would have preached on the need for unity. Consequently, most of us would have failed to address the root issue. And we would have done so because we did not ask the right questions.

Ask yourself the following questions, What are the purpose, vision, and values of the church I lead? Does the core of the church know what the purpose, vision, and values of the church are? Are there any behaviors or beliefs that I have, or key leaders in the church have, that are interfering with our core purpose, vision, and values? What is a win? What is our measurement for success, and is it the rightful measurement?

Church leaders must bring an end to knee-jerk responses to the perceived behaviors of others. The way to do this is by asking the right questions.

Defining Purpose and Success

It is impossible to truly define success without clearly defining purpose. You may refer to something as a success, but if it is not aligned with your purpose, it is not a success. This is a problem, as we repeatedly label things as a success or failure that have little, if anything, to do with our purpose. For example, according to our definition of success, we think our purpose is to increase the size of church membership, or grow the church. But this is not our purpose, not according to Scripture.

Jesus said, "I will build My church" (Matthew 16:18). Paul states, "neither he who plants is anything, nor he who waters, but God who gives the increase" (I Corinthians 3:7). Clearly, according to Scripture, we don't build or grow the church. So please explain why we continue to define success as though we do? Rather than gauge success based on the number of attendees at Sunday service, wouldn't it be more beneficial to apply an alternative measurement?

Defining a different definition of success, not based on numbers, is not saying numbers are not important. One of the books of the Bible is titled *Numbers.* Acts makes references to the number of believers who gathered in the upper room as well as the number of new believers who were added to the church later in the day. Acts 19 notes that about twelve of John's disciples were baptized and filled with the Holy Spirit. The problem is not numbers, per se, but our gauging success based primarily on numbers.

Was Jesus any less successful when ministering to one woman at a well, as in comparison to a multitude of people being fed with two small fishes and five loaves of bread? Obviously, He was equally successful in both situations. Not because of the number of people but rather what occurred with the people.

As the earthly ministry of Jesus came to an end, the crowds deserted Him. Does this mean He was a failure? Absolutely not. But based on our definition of success Jesus' finest hour was His biggest failure. What about Philip? Philip left a thriving work in Samaria to minister to one Ethiopian eunuch in a desert. The number of people he directly influenced dropped drastically when he left Samaria. Does this mean his ministry experienced less success in the desert? Absolutely not. Why? Because he was aligned with the will of God.

Please do not misunderstand me. I am not speaking against numbers. I am simply saying that gauging success based on numbers, and in particular size of church attendance or number of people experiencing the new birth, is a poor barometer for success. And yet we do it all the time.

Furthermore, we use numbers to compare ourselves among ourselves. Those with bigger numbers are deemed to be more successful; those with smaller numbers are not as successful. Paul said people who compare themselves among themselves "are not wise" (II Corinthians 10:12). Our measuring the success of others based on numbers is foolish.

Jesus' success is seen in His faithfulness to His purpose. Likewise, we are successful when we are faithful with our purpose. Redefining success begins with identifying and aligning with purpose.

Equippers

What is our purpose? I address this subject more fully in my book, *Realign: God-Called Leaders and Their Purpose.*[75] I will, however, briefly touch on it here.

Our purpose is defined in Ephesians 4:11-12. Paul says, "And He Himself gave some to be apostles, some prophets, some evangelists, and some pastors and teachers, for the equipping of the saints for the work of ministry, for the edifying of the body of Christ."

The purpose of the fivefold ministry is not found in growing churches or attracting crowds. Instead, the purpose of the fivefold ministry is found in equipping saints for their work of ministry. All preaching, teaching, exhorting, encouraging, and correcting is for the purpose of equipping and empowering people for their work of ministry. The purpose of an apostle is to equip people for their work of ministry. The purpose of a prophet is to equip people for their work of ministry. Likewise, the purpose of an evangelist, pastor, and teacher is to equip people for their work of ministry.

When Paul speaks of equipping others he uses the word *katartismon*, which conveys that church leaders are to help others become what God meant for them to be.[76] Thus, the purpose of the fivefold ministry is to help people perform their God-ordained purpose or ministry.

Notice the focus of Ephesians 4:11-12. Paul is not focusing on establishing whether or not the apostle is more important than a pastor, or if a pastor is more important than an evangelist. Neither is Paul focusing on how each office is to function. Instead, his focus is that of purpose. Paul is defining the purpose of the fivefold ministry, which is equipping others for their work of ministry.

Why then is the focus of so many leaders hierarchical-oriented? Why do some battle over who is in charge of whom? We need to stop such nonsense and align ourselves with our purpose. We are a team and we need to start acting like it. If we truly believed this, we would elevate the teacher to the same level of importance as an evangelist and the evangelist to the same level of importance as the pastor. And the apostle and prophet would no longer be viewed as having greater importance than a pastor.

I think most of us want to align with our purpose. The issue at hand is how do we equip people for their work of ministry? Does equipping occur through preaching and teaching? Are programs the answer? What about special services and events? What about attendance; does faithful attendance generate mature Christians who impact their world? When a person learns to look like a Christian, sound like a Christian, and act like a Christian, does that mean he or she is equipped? If so, then why aren't more Christians involved in their work of ministry?

Although many churches are ineffective at equipping people for their work of ministry, some churches are doing it very well. Alan Nelson states,

> Fortunately, key congregations around the country have incorporated an equipping value into their pastoral philosophy. A robust system of training, on-the-job mentoring, feedback, accountability, and team and leadership development are needed for Ephesians 4 to become incarnate. These churches are seeing 60 to 90 percent of their active attendees involved in roles of service inside and outside the church. Most churches can absorb up to 50 percent of their attendees in internal ministry. But when you unleash more than half of your church in service, you reach a critical mass, allowing your church to impact your community, spilling over in such a way that it gets noticed and thus becomes an outreach effort.[77]

The numbers are astonishing—60 to 90 percent of active attendees involved in meaningful ministries both inside and outside the church! But this is not the typical church. The average church does not see anywhere near these numbers. Why?

Because the average church leader is not aligned with his purpose of equipping people or does not know how to effectively equip people.

So how do we equip people for their work of ministry? Certainly, church services are important, and programs offer some value. But if we rely on programs and think that having good church services is the key, we will fall short in our responsibility as equippers. So what is the answer? How do we effectively equip people?

Let's consider the ministry of Jesus. Jesus healed people, delivered people, performed miracles for people, and preached to people. But what did Jesus spend the bulk of His time doing? And with whom did He spend it? Jesus invested more time and energy in developing and equipping His disciples. Now ask yourself, "What do I spend the bulk of my time doing?" Very few of us spend sufficient time and energy in developing and equipping leaders, and then we wonder why we are carrying the bulk of ministry.

In addition, how did Jesus equip the disciples? Scripture reveals Jesus ministered in the temple as well as synagogues. The New Testament records ten different occasions in which Jesus ministered in synagogues. However, ministry in the temples and synagogues was not the primary source of Jesus' equipping efforts. If Jesus had relied on His speaking in temples and synagogues as the primary means of equipping His disciples, the church would have never gotten off the ground. Instead, it thrived.

So what did Jesus do differently than what most of us are doing? Here are a few things:

- He invested large amounts of time with those He was developing and equipping for leadership.

- He lived what He taught; there was no differentiation between what He said and what He did.

- He empowered His disciples, sent them out, let them fail, and then taught them again.

- When the disciples failed He did not discard them.

- When the disciples failed He addressed the root of the issues, namely that which centers on values.

I have listed just a few things. My point is simple—what Jesus did to equip others, and what we do to equip others, are two different things.

Unfortunately, we have created a culture within Christianity of needy people. Instead of focusing our energies on equipping people we are busy taking care of people. We not only need to align ourselves with our purpose, we need to teach the church what our purpose is. When we have been released from the high expectations of people, we will be able to center on equipping people for their work of ministry.

Aubrey Malphurs states,

> Many churches hire their pastor looking for someone to do the ministry. People are busy, and the other staff is overloaded. The pastors are the paid professionals. So churches hire more and more staff. Which is why you are right: most churches do hire their pastors to do most of the

ministry. Here's the problem: relying on pastors to do most of the ministry is not biblical.[78]

Malphurs is correct. It's not biblical. We must align ourselves with our calling and equip others to fulfill their work of ministry.

Success

Our measurement of success should reflect our purpose of equipping people for their work of ministry. Thus, rather than ask "How many were in attendance on Sunday?" we should ask,

- How many leaders are we developing?

- What areas of meaningful ministry are they engaged in?

- Are they actively engaged in developing other leaders?

- What is the pathway for developing leaders?

- How much time are we spending in developing and training leaders?

- How much emphasis is being placed on equipping?

- How many resources are being allotted for equipping purposes?

Our purpose dictates what we do. So what does this look like? Aubrey Malphurs suggests that based on Ephesians 4:11-12 pastors should be actively involved in the following:[79]

- Pastors should be evaluated on how many leaders they are developing. Many people evaluate pastors on how often they visit the sick or how often they preach. Some churches even evaluate them on whether or not they maintained office hours. These methods are flawed.

- Pastors should have leadership development as a major component of their job description. If leadership development isn't in their job description, it will never get done.

- All individuals serving in ministry should be equipping—not just the senior pastor. Equipping is not the role of a certain pastor only.

- Few pastors should have pastoral care as a primary ministry activity. They should be evaluated on how well they are developing leaders to do pastoral care and to train others to do pastoral care. Senior pastors will never have the time or energy to lead if they are doing the majority (if not all) of the pastoral care.

- Pastors must teach Ephesians 4 in order to destroy the "pastor does all the ministry" mentality. This mentality has done more to harm the church than almost anything else.

- "Doing all the ministry" robs your church members of opportunities to serve. God intends for everyone to be involved in ministry and created each member of the church uniquely to do so. Don't rob others of the opportunity by doing it all. Equip them, trust them, and then start challenging them to develop leaders.

- Churches must require service according to the church's philosophy. Everyone who is a member (and preferably many more) should be serving on a weekly basis. If this isn't occurring, the pastoral staff is likely not focused on the right areas.

Conclusion

Although some of the above may not be doable in every situation, the principles by which the above are based are applicable in all situations. Pastors, along with the other offices of the fivefold ministry, are called to equip people for the work of ministry. But for this to happen a paradigm shift must occur in the mindsets of church leaders as well as saints. Will it be difficult? Most likely, but it is doable. It will require tenacity, for change takes time. But the time and effort invested will be worth it.

CHAPTER FOUR:

PHILOSOPHIES, PRINCIPLES, AND A KING

My kingdom is not of this world.

John 18:36

Merriam-Webster Dictionary defines *philosophy* as "a set of ideas about how to do something or how to live."[80] Philosophies are concepts by which people act or function.

If you want to know why a person does the things he or she does you must first examine his or her philosophies.

We need to examine closely our philosophies. Not all of them are beneficial in achieving our purpose; some of our philosophies are counter-productive to our purpose. One philosophy highly advantageous in equipping people is the open hand philosophy.

An Open Hand Philosophy

D. G. Hargrove, senior pastor of North Cities, embodies the open hand philosophy. He tells the story of how he came to embrace this philosophy:

> In 1986, while pioneering a church in Colorado, I had one of the most eye-opening experiences of my life. I was called to the bedside of a lady in our church, who was dying of cancer. I stood beside her, along with her family, as she prepared to leave this life. As she breathed her final breath, her hands that had been clutched in a tight fist began to release. I could not help but notice that her hands did not merely relax, but they continued to open until her fingers were stretched all the way out and her palms were completely exposed. The Spirit of God spoke softly to me, "The Lord will give, and the Lord will take away."
>
> I thought this was very fitting for the moment, but somehow felt there was more in this message for me. When I left the bedside, I went directly to the church. I began to pray, and the Lord talked to me over the next hour or so about serving Him with an open hand. He spoke to me about letting go, opening my tight-fisted style to an open-handed style. A style that would permit things to come and go from me, and a style that would allow the things I held to grow.
>
> I know the possessiveness that can easily grip us as servants of God. I have felt very insecure

> with my own attempt to gather people and keep them. I have been guilty of tight-fisted living that attempts to hold things. This tight-fisted style is often motivated from a desire to grow, but is in actuality a limiting style. Not much can grow in a tight fist. There is not much room for expansion. This micro-management style of living maintains a tight grip on things that should be released to God, and to others.
>
> In short, I have experienced freedom by opening my hand and declaring, "God, whatever you place in my hands you can move, and my hand is open to accept." I have a lot that comes and goes, but I have learned "the Lord will give and the Lord will take, blessed is the name of the Lord." People will come, and people will go. As we all know, money will come and money will go. I have learned not to fight for things, but rather let things flow through my open hand.[81]

The first time I met Hargrove he asked what my vision, burden, and passion were. After I shared it with him, he remarked that while I was speaking he had been asking the Lord why our paths had crossed. He also asked the Lord what role He wanted him to fulfill in helping me live out God's purpose in my life. Unfortunately, most people do not think like this. His philosophy, the way he thinks, allows God to work through him in extraordinary ways. Hargrove has been instrumental in helping to equip and empower others in ministries beyond the local church. He is a Kingdom-minded leader.

God wants to do great exploits through us. But the extent in which He is able to work is directly related to our willingness to allow Him to flow through us.

Jesus said,

> Do not lay up for yourselves treasures on earth, where moth and rust destroy and where thieves break in and steal; but lay up for yourselves treasures in heaven, where neither moth nor rust destroys and where thieves do not break in and steal.[82]

How do we lay up for ourselves treasures in heaven? One way is by opening our hands. Martin Luther said, "I have held many things in my hand and I have lost them all. But whatever I have placed in God's hands, that I still possess."[83]

Why Do People Reject the Open Hand Philosophy?

The loss of power is a major objection to the open hand philosophy. Some leaders are afraid of what they will lose power or control of if they open their hand. But what exactly is it that we are to control? Does God want us to control people? Are we called to control situations that in all reality are outside of our control? Then why are we trying to hold on to things?

My respect for my friend increased when I recognized he was most interested in helping me achieve God's plan for my life. Can you imagine how this makes me feel? In return, I want to join in with what God is doing through him. His open hand philosophy causes me to want to open my hand even more.

This is one example of how our philosophies impact how we fulfill our God-given call of equipping and empowering others. Sadly, some church leaders refuse to invest time and energy in others when it does not result in the possibility of them receiving benefit for doing so. Leaders are more apt to invest in something or someone when they stand to personally benefit for doing so. But then again, the typical leader does not have an open hand philosophy.

Let It Go!

Diana Nyad, at sixty-four years of age, became the first person to swim from Cuba to Florida without a shark cage. Her 110-mile voyage took 52 hours, 54 minutes, and 18.6 seconds to complete. When asked how she did it, Diana remarked, "It was really rough that first day, Saturday, after the start and I just said, 'Forget about the surface up. Get your hands in somehow, and with your left hand, say, push Cuba back, and with your right hand pull Florida towards you.'"[84]

Much of life is learning to lay hold of, and then learning to let go of, so that we might grasp something else. This is what Paul was talking about when he said, "One thing I do, forgetting those things which are behind and reaching forward to those things which are ahead" (Philippians 3:13). Paul understood the value of an open hand. If we do not learn to let go of things, we will never fully embrace the things we desire.

Controlling Leaders

Do you try to hold on to things? Would you want to work for someone like you? Pastor, blogger, and ministerial consultant Ron Edmondson remarked that he regularly talks with young ministers who feel they are working for controlling leaders. Likewise, I have talked with young ministers who feel the same. Most controlling leaders, however, do not see themselves as being controlling.

Are you a controlling leader? Do any of the following seven signs of a controlling leader describe you?[85]

- People start apologizing prior to approaching you with a new idea.

- You don't really know how people feel about you, but you assume they all approve of your leadership.

- You assume you are always right.

- You enjoy keeping others with less information than you have.

- You think you should be involved in making all the decisions.

- You fear others being in control of a project.

- You ARE the final word on every decision.

The problem with controlling things is that you limit what you control. Controlling leaders create environments in which people with passion struggle with submission. People with passion feel that controlling leaders are always holding them back, limiting what God wants to do in their lives.

If you are a controlling leader then those who desire to be involved in the work of ministry are left with one of two options: they can choose to rebel, or submit and channel their energies elsewhere. Sadly, this is precisely why many church members are not involved in the work of ministry. Instead, they are overly involved in other things, channeling their energies elsewhere. Church leaders who are controlling hurt the very thing they are trying to help.

I once saw a young man ask his pastor for permission to spend church funds for church-related materia . It was a nominal amount. By the time the pastor finished grilling the young man with all sorts of questions, it became clear that the pastor operated from a closed hand philosophy rather than an open hand philosophy. The young man was successful n his workplace, overseeing many employees. He was more than capable of doing the right thing. The pastor had no intentions of doing so, but his questioning was belittling.

This happened some years ago. What do you think this young man's level of involvement has been since then? Beyond faithfulness in attendance, offerings, running the sound system, and a few other things, his level of involvement has been little. He has so much to offer. He uses his sk llset at his place of employment, but not at his church. Why? It is because, for the most part, the pastor is a controlling leader.

We are called to equip people. But we cannot equip others if we keep a closed fist. Ask yourself, am I willing to take a back seat and allow others to shine? Am I willing to let go of some things and allow others to share in carrying the load? Am I willing to invest in developing people even though some of them may fail and perhaps hurt me? Am I willing to play a lesser role and allow others to fulfill a greater role?

Leadership Principles

Donna Prestwood and Paul Schumann, in an article "Seven New Principles on Leadership" that appeared in the *Futurists* magazine, suggest that leaders in the future will need to demonstrate certain principles in order to be effective.[86] The principles are as follows:[87]

1. Know who you are.

We must understand what we know and what we don't know about ourselves. We must assess our resistance to—and tolerance for—change, our fears, our preferences, and our skills and abilities.[88]

2. Let go of what you've got hold of.

In the Industrial Age we were taught not to let go of something until we have ahold of something else. But in the Age of Interaction, we must learn that we cannot move forward until we let go of what you've been holding. Prestwood and Schumann state,

> We must discover the chains that bind us to our past and prevent us from understanding who we really are. Once we understand the chains that bind us, we must let go of them. Letting go puts us on the path to new experiences, from which we gain more understanding of who we are. Letting go allows us to become responsible for our own actions and future.[89]

3. Learn your purpose.

Although everyone has a purpose, not everyone knows what that purpose is. Furthermore, learning your purpose is a journey, not an event.

4. Live in the question.

In the Industrial Age, we learned to analyze a situation, isolate the problem, and administer a quick fix. In the Age of Interaction, we must recognize that everything is tied to everything else. Therefore, we must live in the question long enough to understand the relationships important to a system's solution.[90]

5. Learn the art of "barn raising."

'Barn raising' is a tradition of the pioneer culture where people came together to help someone build a barn. Individuals applied their talents, teams were formed to accomplish specific tasks, and a community was developed in the process. Today's emphasis on teamwork recognizes this basic need to work with and through others. A shared purpose motivates individuals to contribute their energy, skills, and abilities.[91]

6. Give "it" away.

A paradox of life is that the more we try to hold on to something, the more likely we are to lose it. Viewing people as abundant, renewable resources and giving away authority allows the full power of individuals to be realized. The potential of teams and organizations can likewise be multiplied. This is accomplished through ennobling, enabling, empowering, and encouraging ourselves and others. Empowerment fails if it is attempted without ennoblement and enablement first. And it will fail if people are not encouraged to learn from their mistakes. We must relentlessly pursue the release of authority and control.[92]

7. Let the magic happen

The authors maintain the final leadership principle of the future will call for leaders not to be held captive to the demands of their egos. Instead, leaders must become members of teams.

The need for embodying the principles Prestwood and Schumann share is becoming increasingly apparent. The principles are based on the understanding that leadership is influence not position. They remark, "In this highly interactive age, we will increasingly find ourselves in situations that demand the exercise of our innate capability to lead. It is imperative that each of us bring up the leader within us."[93]

We cannot continue to lead the way some of us have been leading. If you are not already embodying these principles, you need to get started.

A King

Many church leaders function from a top-down leadership style in which they act more like a king rather than a servant. According to Scripture, however, we are not called to build our own kingdom. We are not kings. We are called to function as servants within His kingdom. We are to be Kingdom leaders in God's kingdom, not ours.

What does His kingdom look like? How does it function? What is the role we are to fulfill? Is there any difference in church-oriented leadership and Kingdom-oriented leadership, or are they one and the same?

It appears there is quite a bit of difference between church-oriented and Kingdom-oriented leadership. In Acts 1:8 Jesus describes a movement that would start in Jerusalem with a small number of followers. It would then move to Judea, then to Samaria, and then ultimately, around the world.

He says, "You will receive power when the Holy Spirit comes on you; and you will be my witnesses in Jerusalem, and in all Judea and Samaria, and to the ends of the earth." Jesus was casting a Kingdom vision not a church vision.

A church-oriented vision is mostly focused on one's church. Most of the monies collected go to serve the needs of the local church. In contrast, church leaders who are Kingdom leaders "see the four directions of north, south, east, and west and look for people whom they can invest themselves in to accelerate the movement of Jesus to the far-reaching parts of the world."[94] Church leaders who are Kingdom leaders see the church as a worldwide movement. Church leaders who are not Kingdom leaders only see the four walls and the programs of the building from which they lead. Their vision is limited.

I once heard a pastor tell a group of leaders from his church, "I don't care about your burden and ministry elsewhere. I care about my church, in my city. If that is not your number one priority you need to resign your ministerial position immediately." My thought at the moment was he is not as Kingdom-minded as he projects himself to be. In time it became clear as he invested little in the development and equipping of others who served alongside him. His actions revealed he was mostly interested in his kingdom, not His kingdom.

Unfortunately, stories such as the one I have just shared abound. Many church leaders are not as Kingdom-minded as they should be. Kingdom-based leadership is movement-oriented. Church-based leadership is maintenance- and attendance-oriented.

The difference between church-based and Kingdom-based leadership is also revealed in a church leader's mindset when a person moves away. A church-based leader views the move as a loss. A Kingdom-based leader views it as an investment in the Kingdom, that is, if the person moving has grown spiritually during their time at the local church.

Church leaders who are not Kingdom leaders function on a limited view of things. They tend to see the church as being limited in funds and limited in staff. When they look at those they lead they view them as being limited—limited skillset, burden, and commitment. They look at others and think, "They just don't have it in them." In contrast, church leaders who are Kingdom leaders view others, not as being perfect, but nevertheless, as being of great value and having something to offer. Hence, Kingdom leaders invest in the development of others.

The Kingdom

John the Baptist's message centered on the kingdom of God. "Repent, for the kingdom of heaven is at hand!" (Matthew 3:2). After John was placed in prison, Jesus began preaching. His message? The Kingdom. "From that time Jesus began to preach and to say, 'Repent, for the kingdom of heaven is at hand'" (Matthew 4:17). Additionally, during His last days on earth Jesus spoke "of the things pertaining to the kingdom of God" (Acts 1:3).

All total, the phrase "kingdom of God" or "kingdom of heaven" appears eighty-five times, in sixty-one separate sayings, in the Synoptic Gospels. Matthew mostly uses the term kingdom of heaven instead of kingdom of God leaving some to draw the conclusion the Scripture is referring to two separate things. However, there is quite a bit of evidence suggesting the terms are synonymous. For example, in Matthew 19:23-24, the two terms are used interchangeably. "Then Jesus said to His disciples, 'Assuredly, I say to you that it is hard for a rich man to enter the kingdom of heaven. And again I say to you, it is easier for a camel to go through the eye of a needle than for a rich man to enter the kingdom of God.'" Furthermore, in recording the Sermon on the Mount, Matthew states the poor will inherit the kingdom of heaven, while Luke notes that the poor will inherit the kingdom of God.

But, rather than focus on the similarities of the two terms I would like to draw your attention to this simple point—Jesus' central message was the Kingdom. Jesus preached the Kingdom. He defined it as His purpose. "I must preach the kingdom of God to the other cities also, because for this purpose I have been sent" (Luke 4:43). Everything Jesus did was centered around the Kingdom.

George Ladd, in "What is the Kingdom of God," states,

> His teaching was designed to show men how they might enter the Kingdom of God (Matthew 5:20; 7:21). His mighty works were intended to prove that the Kingdom of God had come upon them (Matthew 12:28). His parables illustrated to His disciples the truth about the Kingdom of God (Matthew 13:11). And when He taught His followers to pray, at the heart of their petition were the words, "Thy kingdom come, thy will be done on earth as it is in heaven" (Matthew 6:10).[95]

What exactly is the kingdom of God? Graeme Goldsworthy, in *Gospel and Kingdom*, defines the kingdom of God as "God's people in God's place under God's rule."[96] Anthony Hoekema, in *The Bible and the Future,* describes it as "the reign of God dynamically active in human history through Jesus Christ, the purpose of which is the redemption of His people from sin and from demonic powers, and the final establishment of the new heavens and the new earth."[97]

George Eldon Ladd notes,

> The primary meaning of both the Hebrew word *malkuth* in the Old Testament and of the Greek word *basileia* in the New Testament is the rank, authority and sovereignty exercised by a king. A *basileia* may indeed be a realm over which a sovereign exercises his authority; and it may be the people who belong to that realm and over whom authority is exercised; but these are secondary and derived meanings. First of all, a kingdom is the authority to rule, the sovereignty of the king.[98]

In the simplest of terms, when Jesus referred to the kingdom of God He was speaking of authority. When He proclaimed the kingdom of God was near, He did not mean that a particular place was approaching but that God's power and authority would soon be on display. Thus, a paraphrase of Mark 1:15, which is a summary of what Jesus preached, would be as follows: "God's reign is at hand. God's power is being unleashed. Turn your life around and put your trust in this good news."[99]

The kingdom of God is not primarily Heaven; neither is it primarily what occurs in the hearts of people. It is both. It is here, and it is coming. It is God's reign, His authority, and His dominion in every aspect, in every life. The kingdom of God "touches all dimensions of reality. God's rule impacts actions, thoughts, relationships, families, institutions, and governments, as well as heaven and human hearts."[100]

Living in the Kingdom While Living on Earth

So what does a robust understanding of the kingdom of God teach us? It teaches us "we should seek to live each moment in the reality of the kingdom of God." We are to accept God's rule over our lives. We are to adopt Kingdom values and priorities. These values and priorities are radically different than those of the world. We are to live by a different set of principles and philosophies—His. This is His kingdom, not ours.

Additionally, as church leaders we are to equip people to live and function in His kingdom. Our goal is not church growth. Our purpose is not to fill auditoriums with people. Instead, the driving purpose in our lives is to preach the kingdom of God, to propagate Kingdom values and priorities. Our goal is to live out Kingdom principles and philosophies in our lives and help others live them too.

It is not enough for people to experience Jesus as Savior; He wants to be the Lord of their lives. Lordship speaks of Christ ruling and reigning in people's hearts. Many people are open, and even eager, for Christ to save them. People want to be saved from sin, failing marriages, financial disaster, poor health, and so on. But few want Christ to be the Lord of their lives.

The goal is the advancement of His kingdom. We aren't trying to get people to align with religion; we are trying to get people to align with His kingdom. The goal is not to get people to obey a list of rules; the goal is for people to conform to the values of the Kingdom.

It is imperative that church leaders are Kingdom-minded. We must not be church leaders only; we must be Kingdom leaders. We must live, teach, and lead from Kingdom values. Our lives must be aligned with Kingdom priorities. Our philosophies must be Kingdom philosophies. And the principles to which we adhere must be Kingdom principles.

Unfortunately, the kingdom of God is not on display in much of Christianity. Many people who profess to be Christians are not living Kingdom values. Most Christians are not aligned with Kingdom priorities. The philosophies and principles by which most Christians conduct their lives are not Kingdom-oriented. In fact, there is very little that separates many Christians from those who are not Christians.

Additionally, most churches are not Kingdom-minded or Kingdom-driven. Instead, most churches are performance-driven. Most churches are busy filling up the calendar with little thought of purpose. Few churches are aligned with Kingdom priorities. Most churches are busy doing what they have always done. Few churches are asking the right questions—questions that confront our philosophies. Consequently, many churches are experiencing a decline in church membership, as are most denominations, and many ministers are walking away from the ministry.

Conclusion

The church of North America desperately needs change. And the change must involve a re-examination of philosophies and principles. Many of us profess to adhere to Kingdom principles, but our actions prove otherwise. Furthermore, many of us don't even realize the discrepancies in our leadership. Why is this so, and what can we do about it? The following chapter seeks to answers these questions.

CHAPTER FIVE:

VALUE-DRIVEN LEADERSHIP

But he who . . . is not a forgetful hearer but a doer of the work, this one will be blessed in what he does.

James 1:25

What drives you? Think about it. What is it that motivates you? What influences the decisions you make? What is the underlying cause of your behavior? The answer to these questions has much to do with your values.

In the previous chapter, the importance of philosophies, principles, and the kingdom of God were addressed. Likewise, values are of great importance. Teams function best when team members are aligned with the shared values of the team.

Values Defined

Oxford Dictionary defines values as the "principles or standards of behavior; one's judgment of what is important in life."[101] Thus, values are the guiding principles that dictate behavior and action, especially in sticky situations.

In recent years value statements have become popular, as organizations of all types have come to recognize the importance of values. However, a value statement, in and of itself, is not enough. Alignment with said values is essential.

Values are fundamental in knowing what to do, in helping to define direction as well as stay on track. While interviewing D. G. Hargrove, pastor of North Cities, for my book *Realign*, he caught my attention when he said, "Values drive desire. Desire establishes priorities. Priorities give direction. And direction eventually results in destination."[102]

North Cities, a church that serves the North Cities region of the Dallas-Fort Worth metroplex, is a values-driven church. That is, the church is not driven by performance, activities, or the personality of its senior pastor. Instead, a team of value-driven leaders helps to lead the church.

North Cities is a growing church. However, North Cities does not define success based on numbers. In fact, North Cities is reluctant to talk about the number of Sunday attendees because that is not the focus of the church. Church health, alignment with values, is the focus at North Cities. Moreover, the leaders of North Cities believe that church growth is a by-product of a healthy church, and that a healthy church is a value-driven church.

How does the ministerial team at North Cities function at such a high level of effectiveness? The answer is values. What is it that attracts quality leaders to want to be a part of the team at North Cities? The answer again is values.

Values Are Like a Magnet

Values are like a magnet. Values attract others with like values. Values are also beneficial to defining, and staying aligned, with purpose. Donna Prestwood and Paul Schumann state,

"Real purpose is determined by our values. Habits of mind are developed from values that we have. Values propel us along the path to discovering our unfolding purpose."[103]

Best-selling authors Jim Kouzes and Barry Posner suggest that values create an inner compass for solutions to every problem.[104] Values give members of an organization direction, especially during moments of uncertainty. When a person, team, or organization encounters times of difficulty and uncertainty, it is a good time to revisit, and if need be realign with, its values. Values will see a person, team, or organization through seasons of difficulty.

Values Are Guidelines

Value-driven organizations, whether for profit or non-profit, routinely outperform organizations driven by personality, activity, or performance. "When a group of people are aligned with a set of common values the group will function at a higher state of effectiveness than when simply following instructions, rules, or procedures."[105] Organizations, including churches, that are rule or procedure-oriented, will function at a lesser level of effectiveness than value-oriented organizations. This is not to say that organizations that are value-oriented do not have procedures. But instructions, rules, and procedures are not the focus of a value-oriented organization. Organizations, including churches, which major on rules and procedures tend to struggle in keeping people aligned with the rules and procedures. In contrast, value-driven organizations, for the most part, do not.

Distinguishing Values from Vision

Values are closely associated with vision, purpose, and mission, and thus, are often mistaken as such. However, vision, purpose, mission, and values are different. Vision answers the question, "What are we going to do?" Purpose answers the question, "Why do we do it?" Mission answers the question, "Where will we do it?" And values give direction as to how vision, purpose, and mission are carried out. Drea Zigarmi, in "Just Leadership: Creating a Value-Driven Community" states, "The purpose describes what the company does, and a set of prioritized values gives guidelines for how the company's purpose will be carried out."[106]

Values are crucial in the fulfillment of vision. Zigarmi says, "The strength of vision lies in the clarity of values."[107] When you know what your values are, and are aligned with them, you do not have to be overly concerned with where you are headed. Ultimately, your values will give way to destination. Values are the root reason, the underlying motivation, and the heart of vision.

Value-Driven Leadership

Leadership experts are increasingly taking note of the importance of values in effective leadership. The apostle Paul understood the importance of values in relationship to leadership. His qualifications for church leadership in I Timothy 3:1-12 are value-oriented.

Five years prior to Paul's letter to Timothy, Paul, in his farewell meeting with the elders of Ephesus, warns the elders that the day would come in which false teachers and abusive leaders would arise within the church.[108] Five years later, the very thing Paul warned the elders of was occurring—false teachers and abusive leaders had arisen within the church.

Paul's response was to put in place qualifications for church leadership. Notice what Paul does. Unlike what many of us would do, Paul does not focus on leadership ability or charisma. Instead, Paul focuses much of his remarks on values. Among other things, Paul notes the importance of temperance and having self-control as well as being respectable, hospitable, gentle, sincere, and trustworthy. In essence, Paul declares that if a church leader does not align himself or herself with such things, he or she will be unable to influence others in the alignment with such things. Thus, what a leader is at his or her core is of more importance than what a leader says. Paul is speaking of values. A leader cannot profess certain values and then live out values contrary to those he or she has professed.

Research shows that the personal values of leaders negatively or positively impact leadership.[109] A leader's personal values have a negative effect when they are different values than the organization's values. Similarly, a leader's personal values result in a positive impact when they are the same values as the people.

What does this mean? It means church leaders must lead from a biblical set of values. It means the values church leaders call for others to adhere to must be the same values church leaders adhere to. Unfortunately, some church leaders display values that are self-serving. We can know their values are self-serving by looking at their behaviors. A person's behavior reveals his values.

For example, a church leader may claim that everyone matters. He may point out that the church is a body, and every member has a place in the body and is important. But what a church leader does, his actions, reveals whether or not this is an actual value. To be honest, it is difficult to believe a church leader has a value for teamwork, respect for others, and considers everyone as important as himself, and so on, while he maintains a special parking spot, sits in a special chair, has a picture of himself in the foyer, and the church celebrates his birthday, his anniversaries (wedding and pastoral), Christmas, Father's Day, and so on. This certainly does not look like servant leadership.

My assertions may be difficult for some to receive. Most do not want to even acknowledge that such things may be creating a negative impact. But when we declare one thing and our actions say another, we lose credibility. If we are not careful, our actions will say to others that we matter more than they do. It does not matter what we say if our actions say something else.

As church leaders, it is imperative we lead at a higher level than society. We need to lead from a better set of values. Drea Zigarmi states,

> To lead at a higher level, the needs and values that the leader represents cannot just be any values. They must be the noblest needs and values of humankind—not secular, not idiosyncratic, not self-invested nor hegemonic, nor full of hubris—but needs and values that serve each individual by firmly and yet gently establishing and reminding everyone of the obvious responsibility each individual has to the welfare of the whole. In short, they must be humane.[110]

We are disciples of Jesus Christ. We are called to take up our cross and follow Him. Taking up our cross means we do not have to project ourselves as having power to influence the lives of others. Margaret Thatcher is quoted as saying "Being powerful is like being a lady. If you have to tell people you are, you aren't."[111] As a disciple of Jesus Christ we are called to follow His example of serving others. Our influence is built through acts of service, not titles, special parking spots, or a specific chair.

But what about society's diminishing level of respect for authority? What about submission? If I park at the furthest parking spot, take down my picture in the foyer, sit in a chair no different than others, stop the church from celebrating my anniversary, my birthday, special holidays, and so on, won't I be further weakening people's respect for leadership? Absolutely not!

It may be difficult for some to understand this, but when values permeate the entire organization the level of respect increases across the entire organization. Leaders respect followers, and followers respect leaders—mutual respect and appreciation for all.

The level of respect people have for a leader is directly related to the leader's values. Zigarmi continues,

> If a leader believes that the meaning of life is to gain personal wealth, have power, have authority, or be the one who garners most of the attention, then that will send off corresponding signals to followers about what is fair and just.[112]

The goal is not for you to have great power or authority. The goal is to help people enter into the kingdom of God, to live and align themselves with Kingdom values. There is no better way to do this than for you to live Kingdom values. When you are aligned with Kingdom values you will not abuse the privileges of leadership. Instead, you will seek to build His kingdom and His kingdom only.

Values and Trust

Credibility is built when you do the things you talk about. People are watching what you do, and what you do speaks volumes. For example, you may address giving sacrificially, but if your lifestyle is far above the people you lead, it will be difficult for them to believe what you are saying. Consequently, many of them, especially those who have, will not participate in true sacrificial giving. Why not? Because they are watching what you do more than they are listening to what you say. When what you do backs what you say, you build credibility. When what you do is different than what you say, you lose credibility. When you talk about sacrificial giving and people see you give sacrificially, it speaks loudly that you are a person of credibility. Thus, the most difficult battle in building credibility is doing what you say. The credibility battle is inward, not outward. It is won by aligning yourself with your values.

Most people will never tell a leader they do not trust him. Instead, they will show it through their actions, in ways such as:[113]

- Excluding him from activities.

- Not sharing information with him.

- Not following through on commitments.

- Stress or tension in their relationships.

- Team members not taking risks.

- Team members doing the bare minimum to get by.

- Low morale and productivity in the team.

If you are a leader, and the above is happening, what can you do about it? First, you must take ownership of the way things are. Don't be afraid to admit the need for improvement. Next, understand that improvement first starts with you. Rick Warren, in "3 Fears That Prevent Leaders from Being Authentic and Influencing People," hits the nail on the head in stating,

> Many of your relationship problems are not really relationship problems. They're personal problems that spill over into relationships. Many of your relationship conflicts, including conflicts with people within the church, are really conflicts within you. They are internal battles. If you want to have great relationships and therefore be a better leader, you've got to start with some changes in yourself first rather than expecting everyone around you to change and f x your internal issues for you.[114]

Third, do everything you can to open up communication. "Values-driven leaders and values-driven organizations are formed through meaningful, choice-filled dialogue and action."[115] You will never develop a high level of trust with others without developing a high level of communication. Open communication builds trust.

Zigarmi states,

> The creation of a values-driven community requires a habitual pattern of open discussion. It requires a consistent pattern of truth telling, in which individuals trust that the conflict that occurs in the course of speaking their truth will result in greater understanding stronger

emotional connections, and more in-unison behavior.[116]

D. G. Hargrove notes that the level of trust in a church is a major factor in its ability to break growth barriers. He states,

> There seems to be a tremendous level of trust among the team players in a barrier-breaking church. The trust factor is probably one of the most significant factors in breaking growth barriers. Trust creates an atmosphere where gifts, talents, skills, and anointing can be used to the fullest. Put someone gifted in a non-trusting atmosphere, and watch the limits it will set. We speak of unity, but where there is a low level of trust, there is a low level of unity. Many of the virtues we attribute to growth are produced and nurtured by trust. I am constantly telling our staff, "Good communication creates great relationships, great relationships will produce trust, and trust will manufacture the highest level of production."[117]

When trust abounds, people function in the highest level of giftedness, calling, and anointing.

Fourth, understand that building trust might mean you will have to remove your mask. You cannot act as though you are superman—invincible—and build trust. Unfortunately, this is what many church leaders are attempting to do. Church leaders have become masters in wearing masks.

Jesus took His mask off. Jesus said to three of His disciples, "My soul is exceedingly sorrowful, even to death. Stay here and watch."[118] He was not afraid to be vulnerable, to let others in. Taking our mask off does not mean we should disclose everything. I am simply saying we do not well when we act as though we are invincible, constantly projecting we have it all together. It is impossible to build the level of trust needed for teams to thrive when leadership plays the role of superman.

What does removing the mask look like on a practical level? Consider the following:

- Share the progress. Let others know your frailties by telling them about struggles you've faced, progress you've made, or ways you're mitigating them.

- Focus on strengths; acknowledge frailties. Whiners use frailties as excuses for poor performance.

- Remember, transparency is not thorough openness of everything. Leadership isn't a handholding, self-help group.

- Reveal what is useful. Frailties, shared well, encourage. Poorly shared frailties discourage.

- Let others in. Frailties make room for the strengths of others.

- Some frailties should only be shared with a selected few.

- Maintain optimism and confidence. Frailties aren't an excuse to become a crybaby.

Building trust also means you must remain as consistent as possible. Do what you say you will do. Nothing will destroy your credibility quicker than to say you will do something and then fail to follow through with it. Be consistent. Last, be patient. Trust is not developed overnight. It takes time.

Lack of Trust Is a Sign of Fear

Fear causes church leaders to wear masks. Church leaders are afraid people may find out they do not have it all together. "It is the fear of exposure that keeps [church leaders] from being authentic." [119] However,

> If you really want to build deep, meaningful, satisfactory, intimate relationships you're going to have to let people see your weaknesses. There is no other way. We can impress the people we lead from a distance but we can only influence people up close.[120]

The fear of exposure is closely associated with the fear of rejection.[121] Church leaders are afraid of exposure because they fear people will reject them if they find out what they truly are.

Church leaders fear the disapproval of others. Proverbs 29:25 says, "The fear of man brings a snare, But whoever trusts in the LORD shall be safe." Rick Warren states, "The fear of human opinion disables. But trusting in God protects you from that."[122]

Church leaders must overcome the fear of being hurt again. It is impossible to escape hurt, so church leaders must learn how to deal with hurt.

The truth is you will be hurt in life many, many times. This is not heaven. This is earth where people get hurt. And you're going to be hurt over and over and over. The important issue is what you do with that hurt. If you hold on to that hurt, it's going to strangle the love out of your life. It'll all go away. If you hold on to your hurt it will shrink your heart, harden it, and eventually turn it to stone. You've got to deal with the hurt so you can get on with your life.[123]

Last, church leaders must overcome the fear of change. A leader who is bound by the fear of change will believe it is safer to do nothing than it is to take responsibility. Authors Robert Sutton and Huggy Rao, in *Scaling Up Excellence*, state, "Silence is one of the most reliable signals that people are afraid to take personal responsibility."[124]

We are living in a time in which the church needs to stand up and be what God intended her to be. For this to happen, saints must get involved in the work of ministry, and church leaders must relinquish power and control so saints can fully engage in the work of ministry. This means church leaders must confront fears that keep them from extending trust to others. It is impossible to equip and empower people if you do not trust them.

Insecure Leaders

Are you an insecure leader? Do you seek to control people? Do you struggle with trusting others? Most leaders would never admit to being insecure. Instead, most leaders project an "I've got it all together" stance. Let's take a closer look and answer the following questions:

1. Am I defensive when my ideas or decisions are challenged?

2. Do I maintain a space of distance between those who follow and myself, limiting transparency to only what can be observed from a distance?

3. Do I always position myself out front?

4. Do I seek to keep people under my command?

5. Does my desire to be liked by others keep me from dealing with difficult issues?

6. Am I overly concerned with how I look, the clothes I am wearing, whether or not it is the latest style?

7. Do I strive for positions and titles?

8. Am I always suspicious of others?

9. Do I need to know everything that is happening in my church?

10. Does everything have to flow through me?

It is not uncommon for leaders to battle insecurities. The Bible reveals that leaders like Moses, Gideon, and Timothy, as well as others, struggled with insecurities. What is most important, however, is what we do with our insecurities. We must not allow our insecurities to cause us to behave in manners detrimental to what we are trying to accomplish. We are equippers, and as such, we must be diligent as not to allow our insecurities to cause us to be defensive, distant, or controlling. To do so would be to hinder the very thing we are trying to accomplish—the equipping of others. Insecurities tear down teams; insecurities do not build up teams.

Focus on Becoming

It is difficult, if not impossible, to work well with others, to be a viable member of a team, when driven by insecurities. So how does a person change his or her ways and become a value-driven leader? The short answer is—by focusing on becoming, not doing.

Leadership involves solving problems, and solving problems is important. But most important in the journey of becoming a value-driven leader and leading value-driven teams is the need for leaders to focus on becoming. This sounds simple, but leaders are so accustomed to doing that becoming is often overlooked.

Church leaders typically focus on behaviors as opposed to values. And, make a mistake when doing so. Behavior is what a person does; behavior is not what a person is. Behavior is the outward manifestation of a person's values. If you want to change a person's behavior you must focus on his values. Behavioral change does not happen by focusing solely on behavior. Values drive behavior. Therefore, if significant change is to occur in a person's behavior, focusing on values is a must.

What does this mean? It means "if humans repeatedly act differently from their stated goals, it is important to re-examine the underlying values for a possible mismatch or error."[125] But values are not where the focus for change is commonly placed. The focus for change is typically on what a person does rather than what a person is becoming. Hence, most people, including leaders, go through life learning how to cope as opposed to learning how to change.

Focus must be given to the governing values that lead to counterproductive behavior. The challenge is recognizing the discrepancies between what we profess and what we actually do. This is why focusing on becoming is so crucial. Focusing on becoming involves examining and reexamining one's values. It involves digging deeper than one's behavior and examining the root of behavior.

When Peter failed, Jesus did not lecture him on commitment. He did not talk about his behavior. Instead, Jesus dug deeper. Jesus dealt with the heart of the matter—the values that led to Peter's behavior. Peter had denied his Lord three times. And three times Jesus forced Peter to examine the root cause of his denial. Jesus dealt with Peter's values, not his behavior.

Conclusion

Although behavior is important, it is not nearly as important as values. Values drive behavior. Thus, if you want to change behavior, examine your values. Look to see if your behaviors match the values you profess. If there is a mismatch, determine to become a value-driven leader by aligning yourself with the values you profess.

The likelihood of success in teams is enhanced when the values that leaders profess are the values whereby leaders live. Similarly, the likelihood of success lessens when a leader's behavior is different than the values he professes. Thus, if church leaders are to become value-driven leaders, who lead value-driven teams, church leaders must focus on becoming. Becoming is more important than doing.

CHAPTER SIX:

BUILDING TEAMS

Moreover you shall select from all the people able men . . . and place such over them to be rulers of thousands, rulers of hundreds, rulers of fifties, and rulers of tens.

Exodus 18:21

How do you build a team? What, if any, is the criteria for choosing team members? What attracts people to want to be a part of a team? What, if anything, can you do to further develop a team once it has been constructed? These questions and more are worthy of exploration and are addressed throughout this chapter.

Although much can be said with regard to building teams, the primary goal here is to focus on some of the basic elements that are easily understood but, at times, neglected.

Achieving Success by Building Teams

Jesus placed a premium on building teams and did so because He understood the importance of them. The future of the movement He founded was largely dependent on the success of teams. Likewise, Paul understood the importance of teams.

His ministry would not have achieved the success it achieved if Paul had not taken the initiative to build teams.

Jesus built more than one team, as did Paul. Jesus even built a team within a team. What was the purpose of this inner team? Why did Jesus spend more time with them than the rest of the disciples? Perhaps the answer is found in Galatians 2:9, where Paul explains that Peter, James, and John were pillars of the church. We can derive from this that Jesus' purpose in the building of teams was to provide capable leadership for the church. The early church benefited from the leadership team Jesus built.

Jesus' example serves as a reminder for twenty-first century church leaders. Jesus was intent in His building of teams. We must be intent too. Jesus understood the role teams would fulfill in leading the church in the first century. We must also understand the importance of teams in leading the twenty-first century church.

We cannot afford to allow ourselves to be governed by the needs of the crowd. Jesus didn't. Neither must we. There will always be needs. Someone, or something, will always vie for our attention. If we are not intentional in the building of teams, they will never be built. Instead, we must follow the example of Jesus and purposely build teams.

The miracles Jesus performed caused Him to become somewhat of a celebrity among the people. As a celebrity He had the ability to attract large crowds. But Jesus understood that sustained, long-term growth would not happen if He relied on His ability to attract crowds. Likewise, in spite of the emphasis some church leaders place on becoming somewhat of a celebrity, celebrity leadership is not the key to impacting our world. Neither are programs, worship styles, or anything else we may do to generate crowds. Such things were not the answer for the early church; neither are they the answer for today's church.

I am convinced the success of the twenty-first century church hinges on the building and developing of teams. Success is not dependent on the size of the ministry or crowd. Aubrey Malphurs and William F. Mancini state,

> Jesus' example teaches us that the ministry payoff is not the size of the ministry—the crowd—but the size of the leader's trainees—the core. Success comes in our training a core of competent, godly leaders at every level of the ministry who will take the ministry well into the twenty-first century, long after we've been forgotten.[126]

If we really want to impact our world we have to build and develop teams. Unfortunately, many church leaders are so busy trying to build churches that they do not have time to build and develop teams. This is neither the plan nor example Jesus gave us.

Building Teams

You are a church leader. You understand the importance in building teams and want to build them. What do you do? Where do you start? What are the crucial elements in building teams? Consider the following:

Start with What You Have

I remember when God first challenged me to develop leaders and build teams. It was a defining moment in my life. I wish it had occurred while I was engaged in intercessory prayer, which would make me look better. The truth is, however, I was mowing my yard on a Sunday afternoon. (This was not something I normally did on Sundays).

I was busy, very busy. We had assumed pastorate of a small congregation and were struggling. Teaching home Bible studies, conducting small groups during the week, trying to connect with people in the community, ministering on the weekends, and so on, kept me busy. In addition, to provide for my wife and two small children, I had started a remodeling business. It, too, kept me busy.

The pressure of life and ministry weighed on me that day. As I was mowing I was talking to the Lord about it. (Actually, it was more like complaining.) I said, "I don't have to be here. I could be pastoring a church somewhere that would allow me to be full-time in the ministry. But here I am because I believe this is where You want me to be. And all I have ever wanted to do is train leaders."

No sooner had the words left my mouth then God interrupted and said, "Then train them." To which I replied, "But I only have three to four people to work with as leaders," as though somehow the small number of potential leaders would exempt me from doing something.

Thankfully, God rejected my excuse and called me to align with my purpose. He said, "If you will be faithful with little, I will give you much."

My life changed that day. I made a commitment to engage myself in the developing of leaders and building of teams. I vowed I would not wait until I had ample supply of potential leaders. Instead, I would be faithful with those He had placed in my life and allow Him to increase the amount in due time.

I know this is simple, nothing profound. I am somewhat hesitant to say it. But perhaps someone reading this is where I was—waiting for God to send you quality leaders so you can build a team. Please do not wait. He has already sent them. Start with what He has already given you.

When Jethro instructed Moses in the building and developing of teams, he said, in Exodus 18:21, "Moreover you shall select from all the people able men, such as fear God, men of truth, hating covetousness; and place such over them to be rulers of thousands, rulers of hundreds, rulers of fifties, and rulers of tens." God had already provided; potential leaders were among the people. Aubrey Malphurs and William F. Mancini note, "Based on the ratios in verse twenty-one, and assuming there were one million Jews on the journey, God had provided 131,000 potential leaders for Moses to enlist."[127] Moses' problem, the reason he was carrying the load of ministry by himself, had nothing to do with the lack of potential leaders. The leaders were among the people.

Perhaps your church is small in number. Perhaps you are carrying a heavy burden. Let me remind you of the widow woman, who had just enough flour and oil to bake one last cake, and then she and her son were going to eat it and die. But instead, she gave it to the prophet. The little bit she had was more than enough.

We are often guilty of wanting to live from the top of the barrel. We think access to an abundance supply of resources will enable us to do what we already know we should be doing. But living from the bottom of the barrel is where we experience the miraculous. You may think you do not have enough resources to accomplish what needs to be done. But God has already provided you with what is needed. It is enough. Start with what you have.

Be Faithful with What You Have

What you need is already at your disposal. It may not be enough for what you will need sometime down the road, but it is enough for what you need right now. Whether or not you will have what you will need when tomorrow arrives is determined by what you do with what you have today.

Faithfulness is doing something with what you have already been entrusted with. It is not a state of wishful thinking or a commitment to what you will do if you are given such and such. Faithfulness is recognizing what you have been entrusted with, and doing something constructive with it, over an extended period of time.

Don't expect God to give you more if you cannot be faithful with what He has already given you. I've heard people say, "If I had what a big church has. . . . " The truth is, if you had a big church you would do exactly what you are doing right now. Don't expect your tomorrow to be different than today, unless you start doing something different today than what you did yesterday.

The principle of sowing and reaping is about faithfulness. If you are going to build and develop teams, teams that will help shoulder the load of ministry tomorrow, it will require faithfulness in building and developing teams over an extended period of time.

Make It a Matter of Prayer

In the selection of the twelve disciples or apostles, the authors of the Synoptic Gospels paint a picture that seems to suggest Jesus moved around the countryside aimlessly choosing His disciples at random. That is, except for Luke, who records in explicit detail what transpired.

> Now it came to pass in those days that He went out to the mountain to pray, and continued all night in prayer to God. And when it was day, He called His disciples to Himself; and from them He chose twelve whom He also named apostles.[128]

Notice two things in the choosing of the twelve apostles: Jesus prayed, and He prayed all night.

The fact that Luke records that Jesus prayed throughout the night suggests the choosing of the team of apostles was of no small matter. Additionally, John Gill's *Exposition of the Bible* notes that a better translation of the phrase "in prayer to God" is "in the prayer of God."[129] He further notes that "in the prayer of God" is not a casual or unintentional prayer. Rather, it is "a most vehement prayer consisting of strong cries sent up to God with great eagerness and importunity, fervency, and devotion."[130]

It is interesting to note that Luke makes the point that Jesus went to pray "in those days" (Luke 6:12). To what days is Luke referring?

Prior to Jesus' choosing the twelve apostles, the Pharisees opposed Jesus because His disciples plucked corn from the field on the Sabbath to eat (Luke 6:1-5). Then "on another Sabbath" (Luke 6:6), apparently a short time later, Jesus healed a man with a withered hand, which again resulted in strong opposition from the Pharisees. Thus, "Luke implied that hostility played a part in Jesus' decision to spend the night in prayer before selecting the apostles."[131] In view of mounting hostility it was imperative that Jesus received direction in the choosing of the twelve apostles.

Likewise, we do a disservice to the organizations we lead, as well as the individuals we invite to join our teams, if we have failed to earnestly pray for direction as to whom to choose.

Choose Character over Competence and Charisma

Effective leaders understand those closest to them will have a substantial impact on their ability to achieve success. So what do effective leaders look for when building a team? What matters most?

I would be foolish to imply that skillset does not matter, because it does. Likewise, charisma can be used in building concensus and influencing others. No one wants to work alongside someone who is incompetent. Furthermore, it is much more enjoyable to work with someone who has some charisma as opposed to someone who is a deadpan. However, competence and charisma are of much less importance than character. You can teach someone skills, and you can compensate for someone's lack of charisma, but you cannot teach someone character.

Some are so enamored with skillset that they choose to ignore red flags concerning a person's character. This seldom works, however. Who a person is, at his core, is eventually revealed in what a person does. It is far wiser to choose character over competence or charisma. Jethro instructed Moses to "select from all the people able men, such as fear God, men of truth, hating covetousness."[132] It matters who you choose; choose character.

Remember the Importance of Chemistry

Sports teams have long understood the importance of chemistry. Many, however, choose to ignore it, choosing instead to focus on talent. But this seldom works. Poor team chemistry is often cited as the reason why teams with enormous talent experience losing seasons. When players on a team act in ways detrimental to team chemistry, winning is hard to come by.

This is true for organizations of all types, including churches. Team chemistry matters. I have seen church leaders add team members who have tremendous talent but were not team players. The result was that the chemistry of the team suffered. Seldom does the level of talent acquired outweigh the loss that occurs when the chemistry on the team is affected negatively.

Marshall Goldsmith, in *What Got You Here Won't Get You There,* suggests that interpersonal behavior impacts team chemistry.[133] Thus, interpersonal behavior increases or decreases a team's ability to achieve success. A person with incredible talent may also have a huge ego that could prove to be detrimental to team chemistry, and ultimately, the team's likelihood of achieving success.

Welcome Diversity

Some people believe unity means conformity. That is, everyone must be alike. But this is not what Paul was advocating when he addressed the unity of the Spirit in Ephesians 4:3. Unity is possible because of diversity. If there is no diversity, there is little need for unity.

Welcoming diversity means welcoming differences of opinion; welcoming differences of opinion means welcoming conflict. Conflict is not something that should always be shunned. Rather, it is often something that should be embraced. It is in the midst of differences of opinions (conflict) that some of the best ideas, creative thoughts, and solutions to problems are generated.

When selecting team members don't strive for conformity. Instead, allow for and welcome diversity.

Choose Courageous Followers

Most leaders see the value in having followers who will implement what the leader sees or wants to accomplish. But the best follower is not an implementer. The best follower is a courageous follower.[134]

What is a courageous follower? A courageous follower is someone who has an opinion and is willing share it. A courageous follower will ask questions. They help clarify where, what, how, and why. A courageous follower will share opinions even though they may be viewed as controversial. A courageous follower is committed to the goals and purposes of the organization.

Courageous followers help teams achieve success. Teams do not need "yes" people. Teams need people with an opinion who, with a right attitude and spirit, are willing to share it.

When Should You Build Teams?

For what purposes should a team be built? The short answer is when the task or situation requires a group of people, or when a team might prove to be more beneficial than tackling the situation alone. Consider the following:

Strategic Planning

Strategic planning is a must for organizations to be successful. Strategic planning is beneficial in determining or defining mission, vision, values, goals, objectives, roles, responsibilities, timelines, and so on. The underlying purpose of strategic planning is to help make the organization better, which involves the organization functioning efficiently and effectively, ensuring members of an organization are focused on the same goal and moving things along in the right direction.

In a pastor-centric model of leadership, strategic planning is usually something the pastor does himself. This often results in a less than ideal outcome, as the plan is limited to a single perspective. Additionally, if strategic planning is based solely or primarily on the efforts of one key person, one heart attack can wipe out the key strategist.[135]

Involving others results in a robust strategic plan. Pastors who invite others to participate in strategic planning often limit the invitation to family members (which is not much different than doing it alone) and/or an associate pastor. Instead of limiting the process to a few people who most likely share the same perspective, consider creating a team of a variety of people with differing perspectives, abilities, personalities, and knowledge. A team approach to strategic planning can prove to be of great benefit to a church.

Creative Thinking

Many church leaders operate as though they alone are responsible for creative thinking. Author David Burkus, in *The Myths of Creativity,* however, maintains that "The Lone Creator Myth" is detrimental to an organization's ability to be creative.[136] Burkus says creative insights and breakthroughs are often attributed to a sole person when in reality it is usually the result of a team of people.

For example, the majority of inventions credited to Thomas Edison were actually the result of a team of engineers, machinists, and physicists who referred to themselves as the *muckers*. Burkus says, "There were approximately fourteen muckers working alongside Edison, including Charles Batchelor, John Adams, John Kruesi, John Ott, and Charles Wurth. Many of them have their names alongside or even in front of Edison's on the patents."[137]

Likewise, Michelangelo is commonly known as having painted the ceiling of Sistine Chapel. But in actuality, a team of thirteen artists assembled by Michelangelo helped to complete the ceiling.

Creative thinking is seldom the results of one individual. It is more commonly the efforts of a team of people with differing perspectives, abilities, talents, and gifts who are centered on a common purpose. To increase creative thinking, construct a creative team. Consider allowing the creative team to help design church services, message series, outreach efforts, and marketing.

Starting New Ministries or Revamping Old Ones

When starting new ministries, or revamping old ones, teams can prove to be of great benefit. For example, a team can see things a single individual may miss. I witnessed this firsthand as a team was assembled to look closely at the assimilation process of a church—how guest information was ascertained, processes and systems for visitor follow-up, and so on. As the team drove off the property and then back on to it, the following instructions were given: you are a guest, you don't know anybody at the church, you have arrived five minutes before the start of service, please tell us your experience. What the team was able to generate in three to four hours was astonishing. Together, they were able to see things that as individuals they had been missing.

Evaluating the Church or Ministries within the Church

Bill Hybels is the founder and pastor of Willow Creek Community Church, one of the nation's largest and most influential churches. A few years ago, in spite of a large number of church attendees, Hybels remarked the church leadership of Willow Creek had made a mistake.[138] After a three-year research project that looked closely to see what programs and activities of the church were actually helping people grow spiritually and which were not, the church leadership discovered the programs and activities the church had been investing in were not producing spiritual maturity.[139] As a result of the research, Willow Creek has made substantial changes.

Many church leaders, however, refuse to evaluate their ministry, the church, or ministries within the church. Instead, they are much more prone to continue to do what they have always been doing without any assessment as to whether or not it is working. Furthermore, church leaders who participate in evaluating things often do so alone. A team, on the other hand, can attain a more robust and thorough evaluation of ministries and effectiveness.

A good place to start is to have a team regularly evaluate the effectiveness of Sunday services. Most church leaders would be surprised at the areas of improvement that could be made by simply participating in an evaluation of programs, services, systems and structures, and so on. In addition, teams that have been allowed to participate in evaluating things are more likely to participate in helping to make changes.

Initiating Change

Many people believe that if you build a better mousetrap the world will beat a path to your door. The truth is, that is seldom true. In most cases, a great idea is usually rejected at first.

No one likes change to be forced on him or her. This is the reason why most change initiatives fail. Buy-in must be ascertained from those responsible for change as well as those whom the change will impact. When leaders fail to focus on obtaining buy-in, they greatly lessen the possibilities of change occurring. The beliefs and assumptions of people act as powerful barriers to change and must be overcome if change is to have a chance at succeeding.

Church leaders, in particular, pastors, are usually responsible for initiating changes within the church. However, it may be more beneficial for church leaders to approach change in a different manner. Consider a team approach. Build a team and let the team decide what the best course of action is and how to implement it. By allowing a team to be a part of the decision making process, the chances of success increase.

I once had what I considered to be a brilliant idea for ministry expansion. Thankfully, I built a team that took a close look at my idea. After acknowledging it had some merit, each individual stated his concerns and offered advice as to the best course of action. I listened and, instead of imposing my change initiative on others, I chose instead to build a foundation for receptivity to change. It took more time than I anticipated. However, it was the best decision I could have made.

Building a team kept me from launching a program that would have failed. Furthermore, instead of building a program, I invested several years in building people who would later build and contribute significantly to ministerial expansion.

When Should You Not Add to the Team?

When building a team, and in particular, when hiring staff or adding to a ministerial team, there are some things church leaders should not do. Although the following is not an all-inclusive list, my purpose in sharing it is to stimulate your thinking. Furthermore, while the list may be simple and easy to understand, based on personal observation, it is often ignored.

When It Takes Ministry Away from People

As a church grows, there is a tendency among churches to hire staff to do the work of ministry. This is both unwise and unbiblical. The work of ministry is not the responsibility of the staff. The work of ministry is the responsibility of the members of the church.

When a church adds staff to do the work of the ministry, the church body will believe their responsibility is to fund ministry and to be the recipients of it. Church leaders need to help people understand they are to be participators in ministry, not consumers of ministry. This is what Raymond Woodward did when he assumed pastorate of Capital Community Church, in Fredericton, New Brunswick. When Woodward arrived, the expectation of the congregation was for the pastor to do the hospital visitation. But Woodward refused to take ministry away from the laity. Neither would he allow himself to be sidetracked from fulfilling his purpose as an equipper. It took some time but today a team of about a dozen people from the church makes the vast majority of hospital visits.

Don't add to your ministerial team when it takes ministry away from people. In fact, add to your staff only when a new staff minister is able to "demonstrate that he or she will actually increase the number of people who will do the work of ministry."[140]

When You Add Staff According to the Way You've Always Done It

The world is quickly changing. Technology is advancing. As a result, new opportunities for ministry are arising. Church leaders need an awareness of such changes, a willingness to explore new ministerial possibilities, and an openness to re-evaluate current ministries—both to the congregation and the community. Instead of adding to the staff in traditional ways—secretary, assistant pastor, youth or student pastor, and so on—it might be advantageous to add a technological expert and/or a video/audio expert, especially when considering ministerial possibilities on the Internet.

When a Friend or Family Member Needs a Job

Church leaders need to use great caution when adding friends or family members to the church leadership team. Although there are many positives in adding friends and family members, church leaders must consider the possibility that it may not be the right thing for the friend or family member, and it may not be the right thing for the church at large.

Nepotism—showing favoritism based on kinship and close relations—has destroyed many churches and ministries. While it may be right to add a friend or family member, it is never right to add friends or family members on the basis of friendship or relation.

When It's Just to Copy Another Church

I've seen this happen many times. It usually begins at a large church. A new and creative way of adding and naming staff positions surfaces, and before long, churches all across the country are following suit. Some of the more recent changes in adding, naming, or renaming staff positions include: lead pastor, teaching pastor, family pastor, discipleship pastor, student pastor, catalyst pastor, creative arts director, and so on.

It is not necessarily wrong to emulate another church. We can all learn from one another. But it is unwise to add staff just because another church is doing it.

Conclusion

In this chapter we have looked at some of the elements in building teams. We have addressed some of the initial steps that must be taken, such as the importance of starting with what you have. We have talked about what to look for when selecting team members, such as choosing character over competence. Finally, we have addressed when to build teams and when not to.

I hope something has been shared which will be of benefit. Much more could be added, some of which you will find in the next chapter—the developing of teams.

CHAPTER SEVEN:

DEVELOPING TEAMS

As iron sharpens iron, So a man sharpens the countenance of his friend.

Proverbs 27:17

In the preceding chapter we addressed the building of teams. We now shift our attention to the development of teams, the ongoing process in which teams grow, and what you can do to assist in the process.

While there is much that can be said concerning developing teams, we will focus our attention in two areas: 1) basic foundational aspects in team development, namely that of the development of leaders, and 2) stages of development that teams encounter and the role of leadership in helping teams transition from one phase to another.

Developing Teams by Developing People

When developing teams consider the following ten action items that largely focus on the development of the individual members of the team.

Focus on Developing Leaders

Much of the positives and negatives that occur within the context of teams are rooted in the behavior of individuals. Hence, if you want to improve or further develop teams, you must focus on developing team members.

As previously discussed, Jesus created teams within a team. He developed a team of seventy disciples, a team of twelve apostles, and a team that consisted of Peter, James, and John. Notice the pattern: Jesus placed emphasis on the development of leaders within the teams.

Marshall Goldsmith is a world-renowned executive coach who recognizes the importance in the ongoing development of leaders. Goldsmith notes that he has observed twenty bad habits in leaders that are detrimental in leading teams, such as: the need to win at all cost, the needless sarcasm and cutting remarks that we think make us witty, the need to show people we're smarter than they think we are, the need to share our negative thoughts even when we weren't asked, the need to deflect blame away from ourselves and onto events and people from our past, and so on.[141] Marshall contends such habits are harmful to teams. When eliminated, team dynamics improve dramatically.

Most leaders, however, struggle seeing areas in which improvement is needed. You can help them. You can do this by being an example. Lead the way by participating in self-evaluation. Ask the members on the team for feedback. Ask them to identify your blind spots. Create an environment in which team members will feel safe in speaking up. In doing so, you will help create a culture in which leadership development thrives. Together, you can help each other identify areas in which change is needed, and support one another in making those changes.

See People as God Sees Them

Many church leaders refrain from building teams due to the lack of potential leaders and personnel, as well as the quality of people to work with. The problem, however, is seldom the lack of potential leaders but a failure on the part of church leaders in developing people and in implementing the systems and structures needed for teams to fully function.

Some church leaders view people as resources to be used in fulfilling their vision and ministry. When we do this, however, we limit people from becoming what God wants them to be. Viewing people as resources to be used in fulfilling our vision and ministry means we end up looking for people who fit a certain criteria. In contrast, when we see others as potential leaders, operating and functioning within the gifting and ministry God has given them, and see our role as helping people to develop the gifts and ministry God has given them, it opens up a world of possibilities.

A person's potential will never be fully realized if all we ever do is view him or her as a solution to fulfill a task or ministry we need fulfilled. Bill Easum and Bill Tenny-Brittian, in *Make Leaders or Make Disciples? Yes!*, state,

> Believing every person has the potential to be a leader changes everything about the game. It means you see people as God sees them—a special gift to creation just waiting to blossom into all they can be. This understanding of God's gift to humanity underpins any form of effective leadership multiplication. If we truly believe every person is a potential leader, a totally new world of possibilities opens up for a church.[142]

Recently, I heard of a pastor who was talking about the lack of leaders in his church—a church with an average attendance of six hundred. The problem, however, is not a lack of leaders. The issue is a leadership failure in equipping and empowering those who are sitting on the pew. Correcting the problem begins with church leaders seeing people the way God sees them. Potential leaders are sitting on the pew; church leaders just don't see it.

Invest Yourself in the Process

Leadership development is not about curriculum as much as it is about an investment of self. In many ways you are the curriculum, that is, the most effective way to develop others is to spend time with them. This is what Jesus did. He taught His disciples but that wasn't all He did; He also spent much time with His disciples. His priorities centered on relationships, not programs.

It is difficult to influence others without being an active part of their lives. Church leaders who strive to maintain a distance from the people they are leading, only seeking to influence them from the pulpit, will struggle in developing leaders. Spending time with growing leaders affords them the opportunity to learn from your example. Bill Easum and Bill Tenny-Brittian state,

> Effective leaders aren't the product of reading a book or taking a course or earning a degree. Effective leaders are developed by on-the-job experience and observing the actions of a mentor who are themselves the primary curriculum. As Jesus demonstrated throughout his ministry, leadership development is mostly hanging out with someone who's worth investing in.[143]

While I applaud efforts in the development of leadership training material, I also understand the tremendous value in providing an atmosphere in which people are transformed, equipped, and empowered to be leaders who do God's will. When such an atmosphere is missing, it is difficult, if not impossible, to raise up quality leaders as effective team members.

As a church grows, the need to develop systems in which potential leaders are discovered, and systems in which new leaders are deployed into ministry, increases.[144] Leadership development cannot rest solely on the shoulders of senior leadership. The larger a church becomes, the more difficult it is for leaders to identify potential leaders as well as spend the time necessary in developing them. Thus, the larger a church becomes, the more vital the processes, systems, and structure become.

Regardless of church size, leadership development must consist of more than mere instruction. Someone has to invest themselves into people's lives for leadership development to be most advantageous.

Be Intentional about It

The important things you need to do, but don't have time enough to do, are the things you need to schedule. The things you do not schedule you probably will not do.

Scripture teaches us to be stewards of our time. Paul taught, in Ephesians 5:16-17, we are to make the best use of our time. If developing leaders is of great importance, we must not leave it to happenchance. We must be intentional about it, and being intentional about it means we need to schedule it.

Stephen Covey, in *The Seven Habits of Highly Effective People*, maintains that "putting first things first" is something highly effective people do.[145] In his book, he presents the "Four Quadrants of Time Management."[146] They are as follows:

1. Quadrant One: Urgent and important (crises, pressing problems, deadlines)

2. Quadrant Two: Not urgent and important (planning, relationship building, preparation)

3. Quadrant Three: Urgent and not important (interruptions, popular activities, telephone, perhaps emails and text messages)

4. Quadrant Four: Not urgent and not important (trivia and busy work, time wasters, pleasant activities)

Covey explains that quadrant number two contains the things we need to do but seldom get around to doing. Why? The reason is, they are not urgent.

Some church leaders waste an enormous amount of time on things that are not urgent and not important (quadrant four). But this is not the case for most church leaders. Most church leaders are busy living their lives in quadrants one and three, dealing with crisis (things that are urgent and important), and being governed by trivial things (interruptions, telephone calls, etc.).

Church leaders need to spend the bulk of their time on things that are not urgent but are of great importance. Leadership development is of great importance; it's just not urgent. Will you invest time and resources in quadrant two—not urgent but important matters? Or will you allow your life to be governed by lesser things?

Develop Leaders within the Context of Teams

It is interesting to note the development of the disciples occurred within the context of a team. For example, consider Peter. When Jesus began talking about His impending death, the Bible says, "Then Peter took Him aside and began to rebuke Him" (Mark 8:32). Notice Jesus' response in verse 33. "But when He had turned around and looked at His disciples, He rebuked Peter, saying, 'Get behind Me, Satan! For you are not mindful of the things of God, but the things of men.'" Jesus looked at the disciples and rebuked Peter. Thus, what was meant for Peter was also meant for all the disciples.

This is just one of many occasions in which Jesus developed leaders within the context of the team. Hence, in many ways leadership development is team development, and team development is leadership development.

Help People Discover Their Gifts

You can help develop teams by helping team members discover and develop their gifts. This includes spiritual gifting, talents, skillsets, and so on. Personality assessments, such as the DISC profile and Myers-Briggs Indicator, are beneficial in helping people understand their personalities as well as career/ministry choices. Additionally, an understanding of personality differences enhances the interpersonal relationships between team members. In addition to personality assessments, spiritual gift assessments are also beneficial in helping others develop.

The problem is seldom a lack of potential team members as much as it is a lack of development of leaders. God always provides what is needed. The problem is, we are often too focused on the success of a program than we are on equipping people.

Allow People to Have a Voice

Although instruction is beneficial and necessary, people do not learn by instruction alone. People need to be encouraged to ask questions. The last thing people need to hear is, "Just do it because I said so." As church leaders, we must never allow our position or pulpit to be used to bully people into silence. Instead, we allow people to scrutinize what is being said, ask questions, and embody the change that is being upheld.

Church leaders must be intentional in allowing people to speak up. Just because someone may have a different opinion, and is willing to speak up about it, does not mean the individual does not respect you. Moreover, church leaders must not only allow people to speak up, church leaders need to encourage others to voice differences of opinion.

People, however, will not speak up when they do not feel safe. In the story of the emperor who wore no clothes, the subjects would not tell the emperor the truth. The reason was, they were afraid of losing their positions; the emperor had created a culture in which people were not encouraged to speak up.

Allowing people to have a voice is not only beneficial in the development of people, it may prove to be beneficial in the development of senior leadership. Iron sharpens iron.

Let Others Take the Lead

Jesus first taught His disciples and then sent them out to perform ministry. After having experienced successes and failures, the disciples returned to receive additional instruction. If the disciples had not been given the chance to lead, it is likely their development would have been stunted.

Following Jesus' example, the twelve disciples empowered seven men of good reputation, full of the Holy Spirit and wisdom, to oversee the distribution of goods. Scripture reveals two of these men, Stephen and Philip, were involved in ministry beyond the administration and oversight of needs. It is highly probable their growth in ministry was the result of development they experienced while being allowed to lead.

If you want to grow teams, grow leaders. If you want to grow leaders, allow potential leaders to lead.

Allow Place for Failure

A safe environment not only encourages people to speak up, it also affords people the opportunity to make mistakes while trying to do their best. Darrell Johns, pastor of Atlanta West, in Atlanta, Georgia, told me he was asked by a leader, "What if I mess up?"[147] In response, he remarked, "If you mess up, 'fess up and make it right." Johns says, "If you mess up, we want a safe environment in which we will not destroy you. We want to help you get better if at all possible."

Some church leaders are so intent in making things so perfect, they cannot afford people the opportunity to mess up. These church leaders are more concerned with impressing the audience than they are with the development of people. When development of others becomes the top priority, church leaders will allow people to make mistakes.

I have heard church leaders say, "But they won't do it as well as me." I have also seen church leaders who, though they may never say it, act in ways that portray they think it. And they are often correct—they could do it better. But what is the goal, perfection or the equipping of people? This is not to say excellence is unimportant. We should always seek to put our best foot forward. However, we must keep our priorities straight. The development of people should take preeminence over perfection.

Be an Encourager

Everyone makes mistakes. You make mistakes. Team members make mistakes too. The question is "What will your response be?"

How you deal with the mistakes of others will have a tremendous impact in the development of people. Will you be controlling? Condescending? Will you hold it over their heads and remind them of times past in which they failed? Or will you be forgiving? Supporting? Will you help people get back up and encourage them to try again?

I would like to challenge you to be an encourager. No doubt, you need it. Others need it too, especially after having experienced failure. Moreover, teams are stronger and function more effectively when members feel encouraged.

Joshua is an example of a leader who made mistakes. His mistakes created a need in his life for encouragement. Thankfully, Moses met his need for encouragement.

Joshua's first mistake as a leader (he had previously led the children of Israel in battle) was when he and Moses were returning from Mount Sinai. Aaron and Hur had been left in charge. Aaron, succumbing to the pressures of the people, had constructed a golden calf for the people to worship. When Joshua heard the sounds of worship, he said to Moses, "There is a noise of war in the camp."[148] But Moses, knowing the difference between the noise of war and sounds of worship, said, "It is not the voice of them that shout for mastery, neither is it the voice of them that cry for being overcome: but the noise of them that sing do I hear."[149]

This is the first time Joshua is quoted in Scripture. It is also the first time Joshua is recorded as having made a mistake. Interestingly, Joshua did not go with Moses to confront Aaron and the people. Instead, he entered into his tent and did not come out.[150]

The second time Joshua is recorded in speaking is found in Numbers 11:27-29. A leadership crisis arises within the camp; Eldad and Medad are prophesying. Joshua says to "Moses my lord forbid them!" But instead of disciplining Eldad and Medad, Moses corrects Joshua. Eldad and Medad were not wrong in what they were doing; Joshua was wrong. Again, Joshua was mistaken.

The third time Joshua is quoted in Scripture is when the twelve spies returned from spying out the land. Caleb was the first to speak. He spoke in favor of entering and possessing the land. Joshua, however, was silent. The ten spies with the negative report then spoke. It was only after their negative report had irreversibly demoralized the children of Israel that Joshua had something to say. By then, however, it was too late. At a time in which Joshua should have been quick to speak, he had remained silent.

It appears Joshua's mistakes caused him to become insecure. And insecure leaders hurt the effectiveness of teams, as seen in Joshua's reluctance to speak in favor of entering and possessing the Promised Land.

God, foreseeing the day in which Joshua would assume senior leadership, set into motion various moments in which Joshua would receive encouragement. In Numbers 27:18-20, God instructs Moses in the transferring of power,

> Take Joshua the son of Nun with you, a man in whom is the Spirit, and lay your hand on him; set him before Eleazar the priest and before all the congregation, and inaugurate him in their sight. And you shall give some of your authority to him, that all the congregation of the children of Israel may be obedient.

In Deuteronomy 1:38, God instructs Moses to encourage Joshua: "Joshua the son of Nun, who stands before you, he shall go in there. Encourage him, for he shall cause Israel to inherit it."

In Deuteronomy 3:28, God tells Moses to "command Joshua, and encourage him and strengthen him; for he shall go over before this people, and he shall cause them to inherit the land which you will see."

In Deuteronomy 31:7-8, Moses tells Joshua, in front of all of Israel,

> Be strong and of good courage, for you must go with this people to the land which the LORD has sworn to their fathers to give them, and you shall cause them to inherit it. And the LORD, He *is* the One who goes before you. He will be with you, He will not leave you nor forsake you; do not fear nor be dismayed.

In Deuteronomy 31:23, God tells Joshua, "Be strong and of good courage; for you shall bring the children of Israel into the land of which I swore to them, and I will be with you."

I have taken time to detail Joshua's need for encouragement. I have done so purposefully. I believe it is one of our greatest needs. We all make mistakes; hence, we all need encouragement.

It is very likely that you, like Moses, do not fully grasp the impact you have on those you lead. Your words carry far greater weight than you can possibly imagine. It is doubtful you fully understand how a little bit of encouragement can help to shape the lives of others.

God had to instruct Moses to encourage Joshua. He did not have to instruct him to correct Joshua. Ask yourself, "Am

I like Moses—quick to correct, but slow to encourage?" Your answer may be an indication of how well you develop others.

Stages of Life Cycles of Teams

Once a team has been chosen it begins to experience stages of life cycle. The stages of life cycle a team encounters while on its way to becoming a high performance team are: forming, storming, norming, and performing.[151] Each stage presents different developmental crises that must be addressed properly before a team can advance to the next stage. Hence, an understanding of stages of life cycle can prove beneficial in the development of teams.

The following is a brief description of each phase:[152]

Forming

The forming stage occurs when people first come together as a team. They are initially polite and display positive attitudes towards one another. Conversation tends to be mostly exploratory, as team members attempt to find out about one another as well as the work that needs to be done. Some may be anxious, wondering what their particular role on the team will be. Others may be simply excited and filled with anticipation in tackling the task that lies ahead.

The overall goal in the forming stage is to keep things simple, to avoid controversy, and to fit in as best as possible. In order to move to the next stage, team members must be willing to move beyond "the comfort of non-threatening topics and risk the possibility of conflict."[153]

Storming

As teams enter into the storming phase, members start to get more into the work as well as their roles. While attempting to organize for the group's task, conflict arises. The chief cause for the conflict is the personal relations of team members. All members have their own idea as to how things should be and how things should progress, and behind most of those ideas are personal agendas. As team members begin confronting each other's ideas, sometimes politely and sometimes not so politely, conflict arises. Members struggle in bending and molding feelings, ideas, attitudes, and beliefs with one another.

In addition, any number of the following may occur during the storming phase:

- Member's jockeying for position (especially if roles are not clearly defined).

- Some members may attempt to dominate.

- Some experience feelings of being overwhelmed.

- Most are unclear as to what the objectives are.

- Some may begin questioning the team's goal.

- Some may begin questioning the competence of the leader.

- Cliques and factions begin to develop as team members look for partners with opinions similar to their own.

Many teams fail during the storming phase. Those that succeed and move on to the next stage "must move from a testing and proving mentality to a problem-solving mentality."[154]

Norming

As teams gradually move into the norming stage they are prone to experience an overlap between storming and norming. This usually occurs as new tasks are added and team members have to adjust accordingly. The norming stage becomes more pronounced when trust is enhanced. The level of trust increases as team members resolve differences, appreciate each other's strengths, and increase the level of communication.

During the norming stage team members develop a strong commitment to the overall goal of the team. The objectives of the team are clarified, and the detail of the work is made clear. Finally, feeling more as a team, team members are likely to ask each other for help as well as give and receive constructive feedback from each other.

Performing

The fourth stage of life cycle of teams is the performing stage. Teams in the performing stage experience interdependence in personal relations. Team members are able to work alone, as well as with one another. Friction between team members ceases. Team members genuinely appreciate and care for one another. Additionally, team members are proud to be a part of the team.

The aim of the team is to accomplish the goal or task at hand, and team members work hard to accomplish the shared vision of the goal or task at hand. Structures and systems that have been put into place to help accomplish the goals and tasks are functioning at a high level of effectiveness and efficiency. Synergy is a natural occurrence within the group, as the team becomes greater than the sum of its individual members. Finally, the team is very much aware of its strategy — why it is doing what it is doing.

Leadership and Life Cycles of Teams

Do not expect teams to move straight to the performing stage once they have been constructed. Instead, expect teams to experience the storming and forming stages of life cycle.

As a leader, you can help teams resolve issues and move from stage to stage. To do this you will need to change your approach to match the needs of the current stage of life cycle. The following highlights some of the things you may want to consider in your role as leader.

Leadership and the Forming Stage

The forming stage is generally short lived, but necessary nonetheless. During the forming stage, a leader plays a dominant role on the team in providing direction and establishing clear objectives for the team as well as individual members of the team. A leader must be prepared to answer questions concerning purpose, objectives, and expectations, but must take heed not to overwhelm the team with too many details. A leader should also understand that while some members want to discuss how things will work, others will be frustrated by such talk and will want to get to work in accomplishing its goals. Finally, a leader can be helpful in the development of a team by making sure the members of the team know one another and by helping to draw out quiet members.

Leadership and the Storming Stage

While in some cases a team may experience the storming stage for a short period of time, in other cases, a team may never leave the storming stage. The temptation for some leaders during the storming stage is to suppress any conflict. However, this could lead to a hypocritical team, a team who looks like a team but does not fully function as one. Instead, a better approach is to help a team through the storming stage making sure that conflict does not become a full-blown affair.

What can a leader do to help a team maneuver through the storming stage? Consider the following:[155]

- Establish processes and structure.

- Build trust and good relationship between team members.

- Resolve conflicts swiftly if they occur.

- Provide support, especially to those members who feel insecure.

- Remain positive and firm in the face of challenges to your leadership or to the team's goal.

- Explain the "forming, storming, norming, and performing" idea so people understand why problems are occurring, and so they see that things will get better in the future.

- When beneficial, coach team members in assertiveness and conflict resolution skills.

- Uses psychometric indicators such as Myer-Briggs to help people learn about different work styles and strengths.

Leadership and the Norming Stage

During the norming stage the role of a leader is primarily that of a facilitator. A leader should strive to maintain a balance between focus on the members of the team (people) and accomplishing the goals of the team (work). A leader should also understand that if the norming behaviors become too strong and healthy dissent or disagreement ceases to exist, it is to the determinant of the team. Teams may lose their creativity. Creativity requires conflict. Thus, a leader should understand that a safe environment is one in which team members can be themselves, not one in which team members become like everyone else.

Leadership and the Performing Stage

Once a team is functioning well, a leader should aim to have as little and as light of a touch as possible. The primary focus of a leader in the performing stage should be on the overall vision. Additionally, a leader should seek to delegate tasks and projects while understanding that the team no longer needs instruction or assistance as it once did in previous stages. Finally, a leader should understand that changes in leadership, team members, or other changing circumstances, could cause the team to revert to the storming stage. Unfortunately, some teams never reach the performing stage. For those that do, it takes time.

Conclusion

Leaders should practice the virtue of patience. The development of teams involves growth in multiple areas. Leaders who are seeking to develop teams should also consider the following:

    1. Based on the descriptions above, identify the stage of life cycle your team s experiencing.

    2. Consider your role in helping to move the team towards the performing stage.

    3. Continue to evaluate where the team is in the life cycles and adjust your behavior and leadership approach accord ngly.

CHAPTER EIGHT:

WORKING WITH TEAMS

> *. . .joined and knit together by what every joint supplies, according to the effective working by which every part does its share. . . .*
>
> *Ephesians 4:16*

Paul Chappell, in *Leaders Who Make a Difference,* shares the following story:[156]

> The 1988 centennial celebration in the small town of Bruno, Nebraska, was an incredible display of the power of [teams]. Seven years earlier, Herman Ostry had purchased a farm, including a barn, half a mile out of town. In 1988 when spring flooding covered the barn floor with twenty-nine inches of water, Herman decided it was time to move the barn to higher ground. The $1,500 estimate from professional movers was too steep, so Herman's son, Mike, devised another plan. He estimated that the barn weighed roughly 17,000 pounds. If 340 people carried fifty pounds each, they could simply carry the barn to its new location! Mike

Seventy: Everyone Needs a Team

built a grid of steel tubing around the barn and attached handles for the carriers. On July 30, over four thousand people from eleven different states watched as 344 people carried the barn about 120 feet. Minutes later, the barn was sitting on its new foundation. What one person could never have accomplished alone, 344 people were able to do together.

You can expect extraordinary things to occur when you work with teams. It may not happen immediately—the team may experience the life cycle stages of forming, storming, and norming before arriving at the performing stage—but when it does happen, expect something wonderful. Together, you will generate things the sum of which you would have never accomplished individually.

The outcome or benefit of teams, that which teams are able to generate, far outweighs the struggles and work involved in coming together as a team. Leaders need to be reminded of this. Due to the time involved in forming, developing, and working with teams, many leaders prefer to do things themselves. But while it may be quicker and easier to do things yourself, as opposed to taking the time to invest in building, developing, and working with a team, in the long run it is detrimental to the organization you lead. The church benefits when teams are involved. Furthermore, leaders will never accomplish alone what could have been accomplished with a team. Thus, leaders decide what type of a leader they want to be—one that accomplishes little or one that accomplishes much—by their willingness to work with teams.

Leadership Style Impacts How You Work with Teams

Are you willing to work with teams, to be a team member? Or do you act as though you own the team? Do you believe the role of team members is to help you accomplish your goals, vision, and ministry, while you instruct them in how to do it? Your style of leadership impacts how you work with teams.

Entrepreneurial Leaders

There are various leadership styles and models exhibited among church leaders. One of the more popular styles, especially among those whom many view as being successful leaders, is entrepreneurial leadership. There are many good things about entrepreneurial leaders. For example, entrepreneurial leaders are self-starters, self-reliant, and not content with status quo. In fact, not only are entrepreneurial leaders "discontent with what others have created; they're soon discontent with what they've helped create."[157]

Entrepreneurial leaders are also gifted in inspiring others to connect with a big vision. When they talk about what they feel called to do, it is as though there is a moral imperative to it. Entrepreneurial leaders are risk takers; they see opportunities where others see roadblocks. Because they are willing to do things others are not willing to do, they are able to accomplish things others seldom do. Such characteristics bode well in church planting as well as turnaround church projects—both of which often bring notoriety to a church leader.

Challenges

Although entrepreneurial leaders are often looked upon favorably and are recognized as experts or authorities because of what they manage to make happen, there are some major concerns with this style of leadership. Entrepreneurial leaders often play the comparison game—looking around to see if they are as successful or good as others. Furthermore, they often find their sense of identity as a leader or pastor in how well they compare with their peers rather than resting in their calling. In doing so, entrepreneurial church leaders often place extra-biblical expectations on themselves, and on others, in order to achieve success.[158]

Perhaps most damaging is that entrepreneurial church leaders constantly function from a "got to make it happen" mindset. According to scriptural principle, we are not called to make things happen. We are called to be faithful. The growing of the church is a God-thing. This is His work. His church. His people. Entrepreneurial church leaders, however, struggle with letting go and letting God.

Owner or Team Member

When it comes to teams, entrepreneurial leaders tend to act like owners of teams rather than members of teams. They believe leaders command and followers obey; that leaders determine direction and followers follow; that leaders dictate the vision and offer strategic thinking while everyone else deals with the mundane. But the reality is that people are not a means to fulfilling a church leader's work and ministry; people are not tools to be used. The goal of a church leader should not be to rally people around the leader's vision, calling, and ministry. The goal should be to help others discover their calling and ministry and rally people around the common vision and purpose.

Rallying people around self—that is, the leader's vision, calling, and ministry—is self-serving. Making things about you has never been God's plan and design for leadership. God never intended for a leader to call for others to serve the vision, calling, and ministry of the leader. His plan is for leaders to serve others. One way to know which direction you lean is to ask yourself, "When things go wrong do I take it personal?" Do you think, "Why would they do this to me?" If you answered "yes," you might want to change your philosophy of leadership. You might be making ministry too much about you, and not enough about Him. This is a constant challenge with entrepreneurial leaders, as they often attempt to carry burdens God never intended them to carry.

A Biblical Case against Owning Teams

Paul's concept of authority is often misrepresented. He did not teach hierarchical authority; nor did he display it in his actions. His teachings on authority are deeply rooted in the father/mother discourse of the Second Temple period as well as the education traditions of Judaism.[159] "As such, Paul's concepts and example of leadership were essentially functional rather than hierarchical."[160] His primary objective was not one of maintaining dependence but of supporting the growth and empowerment of others.

Paul followed the pattern of Christ's leadership. Jesus was crucified in weakness (II Corinthians 13:4), "deconstructed hierarchy, and proclaimed a message of grace."[161] Kathy Ehrensperger states,

> To be authentic, Christian leaders have to embody these alternative values and demonstrate their message in the manner of their leadership. The use of power is subordinate to the goal of empowerment. Placed in this context, the idea that leadership means power over others disappears and the tensions between leadership and servanthood evaporate.[162]

Paul functioned from a "Jewish form of parental authority to govern the churches he has founded while also acting as their servant." While at times he issued commands, mostly Paul gave advice.[163]

Why do some church leaders struggle in understanding Paul's concept of leadership as one of service rather than hierarchal? One of my mentors suggested perhaps it is because they were exposed to poor examples of leadership by their fathers. It appears this is often the case, as some leaders would rather remind others of their position of power and authority than assume a posture of serving.

Holding People Accountable

What about holding people accountable? If a leader does not institute rewards, or use coercion, how will he get others to stay centered on the tasks at hand? Better yet, why do leaders think people must be held accountable in order to perform? What is the underlying belief that drives the need for accountability?

> Is it that people cannot be trusted to do what you want them to do? Is it that people fail to follow through on what they commit to doing? Why is that? Is it because they are lazy and irresponsible—or worse, intend to do harm? How did you come to believe people cannot be trusted?[164]

Leaders who place heavy emphasis on the need for accountability should ask, "What experience in my past causes me to believe that, given the chance, most people will do you wrong? What causes me to believe that people cannot be trusted?" If you are a leader who believes everyone must be accountable to you, let me ask you, "Do you have proof to substantiate your belief that people will miss deadlines, fail to achieve their goals, and slack off if you don't keep your eye on them?"[165]

The evidence actually shows otherwise—people want to contribute. People are willing to work hard. People feel better when they are contributing to agreed-upon goals. So why do leaders feel the need for accountability?

Let me ask yet another question—if it is true that people want to contribute and are willing to work hard, why are people sometimes unreliable? W. Edwards Deming, father of the quality movement, offers a possible answer. According to Deming, 80 percent of nonperformance is related to system failures, not the lack of commitment or desire.[166] Furthermore, the two primary reasons for lack of passion are distributive injustice (unfair allocation of resources) and procedural injustice (unfair or secretive decision-making and processes).[167]

Applied in the context of the church the reason people are not achieving optimal performance, or seem disengaged, or seem to lack passion, is because of a breakdown in how the church functions. The issue is fairness—unfair decisions that benefit a select few, decisions made in secret, and so on. When members of the team witness distributive injustice (unfair allocation of resources) and procedural injustice (unfair or secretive decision-making and processes), it is demoralizing. When teams are not performing at the expected level of performance, instead of blaming the people, leaders should first look in the mirror.

Carrots and Sticks

Consider the following scenario—you want to increase Sunday attendance and market the church (make others aware of the church). You incentivize church members to invite people to attend the church. You do this by offering a fifty dollar gift certificate to the person who has the most guests. A few members bring someone with them, but most do not. You are not even sure if the majority of people invited someone to church. Surprised with the results? Didn't think so. Why not? Because "we know that incentives and bonuses are not healthy or reliable ways for people to experience optimal motivation. Carrots simply don't work."[168]

But we know people should be actively involved in evangelism. So we preach on the importance of winning the lost. We preach on commitment. We preach against being so busy with the things of this world that we don't have time to make a difference in our world. We remind leaders that they are examples to the rest of the flock. Some of us will go as far as to tell people if they are not winning the lost they can no longer lead. We institute various forms of accountability in hopes that people will perform at a high level of performance. "The insidious thing about accountability, [however], is that it promotes the use of pressure to get people to do what they probably already want to do—succeed."[169]

Do you see the pattern? We use incentives but if incentives do not work we will resort to a stick. And "the only traditional motivation technique more undermining than a carrot to activating optimal motivation is the stick."[170] "The problem is that leaders don't understand the undermining and short-term effect of carrots (incentives, tangible rewards), so when those bribes don't work, leaders assume it is the individual's fault and put accountability measures—the stick—in place."[171]

Instead of believing you have to hold team members accountable, what if you held a different belief? What if you believed people really do want to succeed? If so, what would you do differently? What decisions would you make? What actions would you take? Is there the possibility that you would focus more on "how to" rather than "ought to"?

Orbiting around the Common Purpose

Many people believe the responsibility of followers is to follow the leader. We were taught this as children while playing "follow the leader." But following the leader does not mean followers are to orbit around leaders. Followers and leaders alike are to orbit around the core purpose of the organization. As long as the leader is orbiting around the core purpose, followers are to follow the leader. But if a leader ceases to orbit around the core purpose of the organization, the follower is no longer obligated to follow. Instead, the follower is to continue orbiting around the core purpose of the organization.

The purpose is bigger than any particular person. Paul said, "Imitate me, just as I also imitate Christ" (I Corinthians 11:1). If Paul were to have ceased imitating Christ it would have been wrong to continue following his example. Purpose holds supremacy over a person. As church leaders, our desire is not to get people to follow us as much as it is to get people to orbit with us around the core purposes and values of the kingdom of God.

There is great benefit in orbiting around the common purpose. "When a common purpose guides both the leader and follower, control shifts from the leader to the purpose itself; we don't require permission to act in ways that forward the purpose."[172] People are empowered when orbiting around the core purposes of an organization rather than orbiting the leader himself.

When the focus is on the common purpose, leaders do not have to be overly concerned with self. Success is not dependent upon the leader's charisma or extraordinary leadership abilities; instead it is dependent upon the clarity of purpose and alignment with it.

Clarity of Goals

There are some generally accepted organizational principles that if not met will result in a team having difficulty in completing its task. One such principle involves clarity of goals. If clarity of goals is lacking, a team will struggle in achieving optimal performance. Research has found that 80 percent of team conflicts are the result of unclear goals.[173]

> Goals provide the foundation for any effective team or organization. Whether they are described as "shared values" or "shared vision," there is some sense of purpose that the team shares. Goals provide a clear focus and direction for the team, an understanding of the current situation, and unify team members.[174]

Unfortunately, many people are unsure what the goals of the organization are.

If the goal is not clear and motivating, don't expect people to fully engage their energy or give of resources. Instead of common interest, people will pursue self-interest. Commitment and effort will be lacking. Team members likely will work alone, rarely sharing information and offering assistance. Team members will not be supportive of other members on the team. Team members will not contribute equally to the progress of the team.

Leaders are responsible for clarity of goals, purpose, and core values. Clarity of mission or purpose of the team is the first principle of teamwork.

> The single most important ingredient in team success is a clear, common, compelling task. The power of a team flows out of each team member's alignment to its purpose. The task of

any team is to accomplish an objective and to do so at exceptional levels of performance. Teams are not ends in themselves but rather means to an end. Therefore, high performance teams will be purpose directed, ultimately judged by their results.[175]

"Anyone who has worked on ministry teams knows that sometimes teams are confused about their mission or purpose and that such confusion can quickly derail the team's unity and ministry."[176] Therefore, leaders must be conscious of the need to restate and realign with the purpose. Teams cannot survive without a clearly defined purpose. In contrast, teams thrive when clarity exists.

Building Consensus

Wise church leaders build consensus. Some leaders, however, resist building concensus believing that people should do what the leader says simply because of the leader's position of authority. But leaders do not lose authority when building consensus. Consensus is beneficial in setting objectives, solving problems, and planning for action. While it may take much longer to establish consensus, this method ultimately provides better decisions and greater productivity. The reason building consensus works so well is because it secures commitment from team members throughout all phases of the work.

How do you achieve consensus? You achieve consensus by listening and brainstorming. The first priority in creating consensus is to stimulate debate. Remember, people are often afraid to disagree with one another, and if allowed to rule this fear can result in a team making mediocre decisions. In contrast, debate inspires creativity.

Additionally, leaders should establish parameters in consensus-building sessions; be sensitive to the possibility of frustration among team members when consensus is lacking; establish time limits during consensus-building sessions; and watch for false consensus—make sure team members have expressed their true feelings.

Finally, leaders should use caution in the pursuit of consensus not to place overemphasis on unity. An overemphasis on unity may result in a lack of critical thinking and debate over ideas. When it comes to unity, the focus should be placed on alignment with purpose, not on making everyone have the same opinion.

Define Roles and Responsibilities

Clearly defined roles and responsibilities are also crucial in a team's ability to achieve optimal performance. In fact, it is often cited as the second most important element in high functioning teams.[177] When clarity of roles and responsibilities is lacking, team members become frustrated with leadership, one another, as well as self.

Roles can be described as areas of responsibility or specific tasks, and may include formal or informal positions of authority. When team members are uncertain as to what their role is, it is an indication of possible breakdowns in the system and dysfunction of operation within the team. Team members need to know who is doing what, who is responsible for what, and what the limits of authority are. When team members have a clear understanding of roles, it makes the team more effective.

Appreciate Differences

Leaders make a huge mistake when they try to get others to be like them—to think the way they think and do what they would do. One of the great benefits of teams is diversity. Differences in personalities, gifts, and callings will result in people doing things in different ways. Diversity strengthens a team; it does not weaken it. When a person does things differently than the leader would have done, instead of trying to change the person to be like the leader, or tolerating what the person has done, the leader should celebrate it. A leader's impact is realized in his ability to work with people, not in the leader's ability to make others like the leader.

Team-Player Styles

Appreciating differences, whether it be differences in personality, gifts, callings, or worldviews, involves an understanding and appreciation of team-player styles. Glen Parker, in *Team Player and Team Work*, presents four types or styles of team players: 1) contributor—task oriented, 2) collaborator—goal directed, 3) communicator—process focused, and 4) challenger—questions the goals and processes of the team.[178] While each style contributes to the team's success, they do so in different ways. It is important to remember that although a person may be different in what he or she has to offer the team, each person is valuable to the overall success of the team.

Below is a brief overview of each style of team player. Notice the benefit of each style actively involved in the success of a team.

Contributor

Contributors are focused on the short-term task. This style of a team player likes a detailed plan of action; is organized, dependable, and timely; likes to provide data and information to the rest of the team; is tactical; likes to analyze and study things in detail before moving forward; and expects others to share their high expectations of quality work.

Collaborator

Collaborators are focused on the goal of the team, the team's overall mission and vision. They also help teams understand the role they fulfill in the larger strategy of an organization. Collaborators tend to be cooperative, flexible, confidant, visionary, and imaginative.

Communicator

Communicators care about how well people work together, which largely involves how people communicate with each other. Communicators are facilitators as well as consensus builders. They encourage team members to participate in discussion and involvement. They pull others into conversations and processes. Communicators help others resolve conflict, and often do so through the use of humor. Communicators are "supportive, encouraging, relaxed, tactful, helpful, friendly, patient and spontaneous."[179]

Challenger

Challengers ask tough questions. They question what the team is doing; they question how well the team is performing. Challengers are also willing to disagree with others, including leaders. Although challengers are often viewed as being negative, they are of great value to the overall success of a team. They are willing to be candid, open, and honest. In doing so challengers help teams achieve things they would never achieve otherwise. Challengers help push teams to greater levels of creativity and innovation. They are not afraid to move in directions that involve risks.

Weaknesses of Each Team-Player Style

Although each style offers an array of possible contributions, each style is not without possible negatives. For example, contributors have to guard against becoming so focused on details that they forget the overall purpose. They can impose too much information and data on the team, overanalyze a situation or problem, and reject possible solutions as not being good enough. They can also be guilty of wasting time and resources on things that are not needed.

Collaborators have to be careful not to become overcommitted, insensitive, over involved, and overambitious. They can also become so visionary that they overlook practical matters and important details that are essential in making the vision a reality. Collaborators can become so focused on tomorrow that they overlook what needs to be done today in order for tomorrow to become a reality.

Communicators have to guard against being overly appeasing, impractical, and manipulative. They must also take caution not to become so focused on getting people to get along with one another that they lose sight of the goal. Also, communicators must understand that constructive conflict can be of great benefit in creativity and generating desirable results.

Finally, challengers must be careful not to push too far and argue about things long after consensus has been reached. Challengers also need to be aware of the fact that others will stop listening to them if they appear constantly to be in opposition to what the team is trying to do. Finally challengers must be careful not to pick fights or disagreements simply because they enjoy it.

Interpersonal Relationships

Interpersonal relationships among team members are a chief factor in a team's ability to achieve success. The quality of relationship between two people largely determines the level of influence and contribution each will have with one another. Unfortunately, many teams fail to reach full potential because of interpersonal relationship issues.[180]

Problems can occur in a variety of ways, such as: problems when team players use their strengths to excess and problems when team members become intolerant of other members due to differences in personalities and gifting. Leaders must help team members understand and appreciate each other. Again, as has previously been stated, personality assessments and profiles, such as DISC and Myers-Briggs, can be beneficial in helping people understand each personality's strengths and challenges.

Team members must also be careful not to take advantage of one another. Some ways in which team members can take advantage of others are frequent absences, lack of participation, failing to complete assignments, low energy during meetings, blaming others instead of taking responsibility, and showing up late.

Leaders must take an active role in addressing such matters. Interpersonal relationship issues can demoralize a team. Indeed, poor team chemistry is often the defining factor in a team achieving success or struggling to perform. It is the leader's responsibility to help team members grow in interpersonal relationships.

Communication

If teams are going to achieve success, communication is a must.

If the team cannot communicate then it is impossible for it to develop and compete either its social tasks or its technical tasks. Teams must understand communication channels, their linkage with other parts of the organization and how they prioritize the sharing of important information.[181]

Communication helps to generate trust, and trust is the most important element an organization has. People will not participate fully when the level of trust is low. In contrast, when the level of trust is high people are more likely to participate fully.

The leader's style of communication influences the interaction of the entire group and is critical to building trust. A leader who listens and provides timely feedback creates an environment where communication is encouraged and valued.[182] Any leader, who remains aloof, is difficult to get ahold of, and withholds information vital to a team's success will cause others to distrust him. For trust to increase, trust must be given. Communication is a must in increasing levels of trust.

Conflict

Conflict involves the interaction with team members during times of dispute or disagreement. While it is one thing to disagree, it is another to be disagreeable. Conflict, in and of itself, is not necessarily wrong. Being disagreeable is wrong. Conflict is a natural part of teams working together. Differences of opinion will arise. However, when conflicts cannot be resolved, tension between team members may intensify, and team members may begin to make personal attacks or aggressive gestures to one another.

Leaders must not allow any one individual to dominate others, or allow certain individuals to withdraw from full participation. Team members must be taught the proper manner in dealing with unhealthy conflict—blessed are the peacemakers, not peace seekers.

Bullies

Gary and Ruth Namie, in *The Bully at Work*, claim that 95 percent of the workforce has seen bullying at work at least once.[183] Although I am unaware of any data concerning bullying in churches, it does exist. Bullying occurs in forms of intimidation, intentionally withholding information or resources critical to performance, purposeful humiliation, gossip, and slander.

Leaders have a responsibility to confront bullies and put a stop to their bullying. Bullying must not be allowed to exist. One of the problems with bullying is that it always escalates. Eventually, it will result in negative impact on the productivity and efficiency of a team. Bullying also has a negative impact in the social dynamics of a group.

Leaders may choose to avoid or ignore bullying, but this does not make it go away. Wise leaders see what is happening, intervene, and put a stop to it. It is not the responsibility of the person who is being bullied to deal with it on his or her own; it is the responsibility of the leader. The success of teams is hindered when bullying is tolerated.

Code of Conduct

One tool known to strengthen interpersonal relationships is a code of conduct. A code of conduct, with specific agreements about how team members will treat each other, can help team members develop stronger emotional bonds with each other.

A code of conduct might include such things as: respecting commitments; time consciousness; valuing differences of opinions; appreciating differences of personalities, gifts, and callings; supporting one another; keeping confidential matters confidential; honoring and supporting group decisions; sharing differing opinions in a respectful manner; and being careful when using humor.

Discussions concerning such matters can prove beneficial for teams, as members get to know one another at a deeper level. In doing so, teams are able to establish norms that ensure efficiency and success.

Value the Personal Lives of Team Members

Church leaders must not view teams as tools to perform ministry. People have lives. They have homes, marriages, children, and jobs. They have responsibilities beyond the four walls of the church. Involvement does not equal spirituality; just because a person may be busy with ministry responsibilities does not mean that everything is well in his or her life.

Some church leaders have unrealistic expectations for others. Instead of jumping to conclusions and labeling people as uncaring, or lacking commitment, leaders should ask, "Is the workload too heavy? Are the expectations overbearing and filled with meaningless tasks? Are the expectations clear and precise?" Leaders also need to remember that team members may not be as flexible with time and schedule as the leader may be.

Finally, leaders who care about team members will know the passions, gifting, dreams, and callings of team members. They will be attuned with the hurts, pains, and struggles of team members. In short, worthy leaders value the personal lives of team members. They do not use people for personal gain.

Make Ministry Fun

Leaders who are able to make ministry fun are able to attract people to the cause. Recently, I was told of someone who had transferred to a growing and thriving church. After a few months the man approached the pastor and said, "I've been trying to figure out what is different about this church. I think I know. You all have put the fun back into ministry."

Church business, that is, influencing and changing lives of others for the better, is a serious business. However, that does not mean it is impossible to have fun in ministry. Wise leaders understand there is a time for everything, including laughter. They do not take themselves seriously, even though they work hard. They know how to make ministry fun and work to create environments in which teams have fun.

Pray Together

Prayer was never meant to be a one-man thing. This is not to say that a single person cannot or should not pray. It is simply to say that prayer is a powerful team activity in which church leaders should seriously consider participating.

On numerous occasions Jesus prayed with the team of twelve as well as the team of three. He participated in lengthy prayer meetings with His team, even when they had trouble staying awake. Not only did Jesus talk about prayer, He demonstrated prayer. If Jesus deemed it necessary to pray together as a team, it stands to reason we should too.

Be Supportive

Team members need to feel they will be supported when they step out and try things. People are less likely to attempt new things unless they feel they will be supported when doing so. Team members are robbed of growth and development when they are not allowed to experience the joys of success or pain of failure that comes from attempting new things.

Team members should feel that if things do not work as planned, that you, the leader, will be supportive and appreciate the effort. More focus should be placed on the development of people rather than the outcome of their performance. Applaud effort. Applaud alignment with values. Applaud the willingness to try things. Recognize the value of an opportunity to learn from a mistake.

Church leaders who cannot afford people the opportunity to take risk stunt the growth and development of others. Wise leaders, however, encourage risk taking and continuous learning, even though it may involve mistakes. The possibility for the extraordinary increases when teams feel supported in risk taking.

Conclusion

Working with teams involves much more than what is covered here. However, it is my hope that something has been shared that will be of benefit to you and your team. Working with teams requires patience, resilience, and flexibility, but it is worth the effort. Remember, you are not to function as the owner of the team; you are a team member. When you act like an owner you will end up with team members who act like employees. If you really want to work with a team, you must give up ownership and become a member of it.

CHAPTER NINE:

EMPOWERING TEAMS

The works that I do he will do also; and greater works than these he will do.
John 14:12

Empowerment is a buzzword today in many circles, including churches, but not everyone who uses the term understands what empowerment means. Some seem to think empowerment is delegation, failing to differentiate the difference between the two words. But empowerment is not delegation.

The word *power* is at the center of the word empowerment and is the essence of empowerment. *Merriam-Webster Dictionary* defines *empowerment* as the act of giving away power or authority.[184] Empowerment is a leader sharing himself—his influence, position, power, and opportunities—with others, with the purpose of investing in their lives so they can function at their best.

Church leaders empower others when they invite others to participate in shared ministry and shared vision. They also empower them when they share with them resources, knowledge, power, and authority needed for success. Empowerment is about believing in others and helping them succeed. It is about removing unnecessary bureaucratic boundaries that limit the accessibility people have to what they need. Empowering teams means letting go of things and allowing others to assume responsibility.

Tony Morgan, in *Developing a Theology of Leadership*, says,

> We as church leaders don't tell people what to do to accomplish the vision. Instead, we help people discover their spiritual giftedness and free them to use these gifts to fulfill the vision. It's not delegation, because with delegation I'm still responsible. It's empowerment.[185]

Empowering Leadership

Authority is something that should be shared, not something that should be imposed. If leadership is not being released to others, can you truly call it leadership?[186] The focus of authority should not be on submission to it but rather the benefit of sharing it with others. This is the point that is often overlooked in Luke 7:7-8.

> Say the word, and my servant will be healed. For I also am a man placed under authority, having soldiers under me. And I say to one, "Go," and he goes; and to another, "Come," and he comes; and to my servant, "Do this," and he does it.

If we fail to empower others, we have failed to fulfill our God-given call of equipping people for their work of ministry.

Some leaders would rather hold on to power than to extend power. Such leaders have faulty philosophies, have major insecurities, are self-focused, or just simply do not understand the purpose of leadership. In contrast, leaders who empower people believe:

> It's less about the leader and more about the God-ordained vision. It's less about the leader and more about those being led. It's less about the leader and more about synergy of the body.[187]

Leaders often resist and at times refrain from empowering others because they see the imperfection in others. They are afraid if they extend power to someone else the person will make a mistake. But what is the goal? What is the purpose? Is it to display perfection or equip people?

"It often takes more work, investment of time, and trust in God to empower others to participate in important leadership functions. But the rewards and results of such empowerment are exponentially greater."[188] Shane Sokoll, in "Are You an Empowered, Empowering Leader," says, "Kingdom expansion is present in believers; empowerment is one key to releasing the potential."[189]

Kingdom expansion occurs when leaders empower others. Leaders cannot be afraid to empower people. The apostle Paul founded a church in Thessalonica and ordained elders to oversee it, all within a three-month period. He did not wait for perfection before empowerment.

Mark Barrick, pastor of Cypress Grove Fellowship in Orlando, Florida, also planted a church in Courjolles, Haiti. While visiting some of his saints' family in Haiti, Barrick taught a Bible study that resulted in the baptism of a few people, including twenty-four-year-old Sauvenel. With no church nearby, and Barrick not scheduled to return for several months, he presented his notes to Sauvenel and asked him to teach from them until he returned. Barrick empowered Sauvenel. In time, Barrick was able to connect Sauvenel with the resident missionary, Ron Brian, who operates a Bible college in Haiti. Today, there is a growing church in Courjolles, Haiti, largely because someone was willing to empower another.

Empowerment is a value-driven issue. According to Ken Blanchard, John Carlos, and Alan Randolph, in *Empowerment Takes More Than a Minute*, people already possess much of what is needed for them to succeed; they just need permission to act on it.[190] Leaders, who value such things as equipping and developing teams, empower people; those who value self-preservation do not.

Instead of leaders viewing the act of empowering others as a loss of power, they should view it as an opportunity to experience a new level of leadership. Instead of directing and controlling, leaders are able to help coordinate efforts, distribute resources, coach others to become more effective, and so on. Empowerment, in many ways, leads to a role reversal. Instead of people working for the leader, the leader now works or serves the people. This certainly seems what Jesus had in mind when He said,

> The kings of the Gentiles exercise lordship over them, and those who exercise authority over them are called "benefactors." But not so among you; on the contrary, he who is greatest among you, let him be as the younger, and he who governs as he who serves. For who is greater, he who sits at the table, or he who serves? Is it not he who sits at the table? Yet I am among you as the One who serves.[191]

Empowering Put into Practice

How do you empower someone? What does empowering someone consists of? Blanchard, Carlos, and Randolph present three keys to empowerment.[192] The first key consists of leaders sharing information with others. Sharing sensitive information with others means you trust them, and trust is essential in empowering others.

The second key involves creating autonomy through boundaries. Boundaries consist of the values, goals, and organizational systems of an organization. Creating autonomy through boundaries simply means that the values and goals must be so clear that a person is able to see the role they fulfill in the big picture and know how to act towards it. Moreover, when people are able to see how their part helps to complete the big picture, they will feel their contribution is valuable. This is what makes vision come alive.

The third key is to replace command and control, hierarchy leadership, with self-directed teams. Such teams allow everyone to participate in planning and performing and help the organization to become healthy and experience growth.

According to research, leaders empower others when they actively practice five behaviors: 1) leading by example, 2) coaching, 3) participative decision-making, 4) informing, and 5) showing concern/interacting with the team.[193] Here is a brief overview of each behavior:[194]

1. Leading by example is demonstrating—through action—the leader's commitment to developing and empowering the team. It involves communication, openness, feedback, and professionalism.

2. Coaching refers to a set of behaviors that develop the team members' talents by improving their self-awareness. It includes exploring a team member's ideas about performance improvements to help the team be more self-reliant.

3. Participative decision-making means eliciting team members' participation in planning and decision-making activities. This includes encouraging team members to express their ideas and opinions.

4. Informing refers to the leader's dissemination of timely and accurate information about goals, performance, the larger organization's strategy, and other important issues.

5. Showing concern/interacting with the team is a collection of behaviors that communicate a regard for the team's morale and contribution of the team as a whole. This includes taking time to discuss team members' concerns, monitoring the team's activities and work, and patient explaining.

Clearly, empowering others does not occur in a vacuum. That is, it doesn't happen minus the involvement of a leader. For empowerment to occur, leaders must be actively engaged in the process.

If a leader does not have the values for empowering others, he will not participate in empowering others. The values of a leader drive the behaviors of a leader, and the behaviors of a leader determine whether or not a leader empowers others. If a leader does not value the growth and development of people, if he does not value the callings, gifts, and ministry of people, it does not matter what forms or practices are put in place for developing people, he will constantly fall short in empowering people.

Are You an Empowering Leader?

For a team to fully function, it must be empowered to do so. The power and impact of a team can never be completely and entirely known until the team has been empowered. This means team members must feel safe to act and perform without constant fear of being corrected for not doing things the way the leader would do them. It also means leaders must refrain from meddling with things.

Some leaders are quick to delegate things, thinking that by delegating things to people they are empowering people. But delegation is not the same thing as empowerment. One of the chief differences between delegation and empowerment is that delegation tends to cause people to feel as though they are performing a job. In contrast, empowerment causes people to feel a part of the team. Sadly, many church leaders talk about delegation; few leaders truly empower others.

People are waiting to be empowered. The reason some leaders lack volunteers is because of their failure to empower people. The reason some leaders bemoan the lack of responsible leaders is because of their failure to empower people. The reason some leaders do not have a high-performing team to work with is because of their failure to empower people. And the reason some leaders struggle in empowering others is because of insecurities. Insecure leaders are controlling leaders,

Seventy: Everyone Needs a Team

and while controlling leaders may delegate things to others, they will never empower others.

The reason marketplace leaders remain uninvolved in the church is because leaders will not empower them. People who display great leadership skills daily in the marketplace have much to offer the church. But in many churches marketplace leaders are never empowered to function within their gifting. This needs to change so the church can be what God intends her to be.

If church leaders want to lead churches that produce leaders, church leaders are going to have to empower leaders. What is the difference between empowered people and people who have been delegated responsibilities? Empowered people . . .

- Know you believe in them.

- Know what a win looks like; the goal is clear.

- Do not have to ask for permission to act.

- Do not live in a constant state of fear of making a mistake.

- Know you will back the decisions they make.

- Have access to the resources needed to succeed.

- Share in the rewards that come with success.

Empowerment and Succession

The lack of empowerment is a leading reason why succession often fails. Consider Alexander the Great (356-323 BC), arguably the world's greatest military strategist, tactician, and ruler. His achievements have influenced and inspired leaders of all types for hundreds of years. Yet in spite of his achievements, Alexander the Great was not without his share of leadership faults, one of which was his failure to empower others.

Partha Bose, in *Alexander the Great's Art of Strategy,* suggests the reason Alexander refrained from empowering others was because he was afraid it would result in a challenge to his supremacy.[195] Bose states that toward the end of Alexander's rule, "he frequently selected people for senior positions because of their loyalty or record of service toward him—not necessarily due to their ability to lead people or win battles."[196]

When stricken with a fatal illness at the age of thirty-two, his top generals gathered around him, concerned that there was no succession plan in place. When asked to whom he desired to leave his kingdom he obscurely said, "To the strongest."[197] It is ironic that a leader who had a plan for conquering nations would not have a plan for succession. But then again, such is the nature of a person who does not empower others.

Do you have a plan for succession? What about the leaders who serve in your organization? If not, the first step is to begin empowering people.

Moses and Joshua

Moses' empowering Joshua was a key component in the succession that took place between the two leaders. Moses was instrumental in the development of Joshua's leadership skills. He allowed Joshua to serve in a leadership role. He willingly shared his authority with Joshua so that the people would begin to follow him. He endorsed Joshua in front of the people. And he strengthened and encouraged Joshua on numerous occasions. Lastly, when the time came, Moses stepped aside, allowing Joshua to assume leadership.

Likewise, Jesus empowered His disciples. In doing so, He laid the foundation for successful succession.

> Almost from the first day He was with them, Jesus told His followers that He would be with them only a short time. From time to time they argued with Him about the limited tenure He described, but He continued to reiterate that it was right for Him to go. From the beginning, He prepared them for life when He was gone. He modeled how to depend on the Holy Spirit and impact others.[198]

The most successful leadership successions occur when leaders are actively involved in empowering others.

How Teams Can Impact Succession

Larry Osborne and Chris Brown offer an interesting concept with regards to succession. Osborne is the founding pastor of North Coast Church, a multi-campus church in California, and Brown serves as co-senior pastor. In an article, titled "No More One-Man Band," Osborne and Brown describe how North Coast has transitioned into a model of shared leadership that has made pastoral succession, from their perspective, obsolete.[199] Osborne remarks,

> Almost 25 years ago, I started sharing the pulpit with multiple other pastors. While many churches run like a sole proprietorship (senior pastor) with valued employees (even including other pastors in so-called "shared leadership"), I wanted a true partnership—like in a law firm.[200]

Eventually, the practice of sharing in ministry led to a team of senior pastors that "promote healthy margins, and stability for the pastors and the church."[201]

Although the concept of a team of senior pastors is foreign to many, it offers some tremendous benefits. One of the benefits is being able to fully utilize a person's leadership gifts, particularly when they are senior pastor gifts. In the traditional model of senior pastor, only one person can exhibit senior pastor gifting. Others with the same gifts are left with two choices: suppress the gifts, or go somewhere else and be the sole senior pastor.

Another benefit is it contributes to a strong team instead of the way many successions turn out. Many successions do not turn out well. Often, the senior pastor gets his energy back and feels he can continue into his nineties. Meanwhile, the pastor-to-be is wishing the senior pastor would move off the scene.

The problem with the traditional model of succession is the very definition of succession. Brown says, "By definition succession means someone has to step away. That's not always healthy or natural. Sharing is much better."[202] He goes on to state that the benefit of a team of senior pastors is that it allows veteran pastors to enter into "one of the most fruitful stages of their life."[203]

Yet another benefit of a team of leaders is the freedom that comes with it. Brown states, "Sharing leadership gave me a life."[204] It frees you up to spend quality time with your family; to pursue ministerial callings and gifting that could not happen if you were the only senior leader. It also helps to alleviate stress and eliminate burnout.

There are challenges, however, some of which are frustrating, such as the extent of communication that is required for the model to work effectively. But perhaps one of the biggest challenges involves giving up ownership or the desire for ownership. Osborne maintains that when a person loses any of the three Ps—power, prestige, and preference—and gets upset, the person is dealing with a spiritual issue.[205] He states,

> This is the crux of what makes transitions such a dangerous time for a church. It's why a former deacon or elder leaves the church—they no longer have influence like they once did. It's why as church plants grow, they consistently have their little coup attempt because "Aaron" and "Miriam" are asking, "Why do you get all the prestige?"[206]

My purpose in sharing this model is not to suggest it should be duplicated in all situations. I simply offer it for the following reasons: 1) to make the point that the traditional model for succession is filled with flaws and challenges and seldom works well, and 2) an alternative model, such as a team of leaders, is a viable solution to succession.

Empower Those Who Serve

Leaders should only empower those who are willing to serve, not those who are looking for positions to display authority and power. How do you know if a person has the right motives for leadership? Look to see if the person is serving.

Joshua was serving when Moses empowered him. Exodus 24:13 refers to Joshua as Moses' assistant. The word assistant could also be translated as servant. Joshua, who is first mentioned in Scripture as the commander of the army of Israel, served or assisted Moses. "Joshua, a man who would later lead the conquest of the Promised Land, did not think it beneath him to be the servant, the burden bearer, of Moses."[207]

Leaders make a mistake when promoting a person to a position of authority in hopes the person will become something he is not. For example, if a person does not show signs of being responsible when he does not have a title, it is doubtful he will suddenly become responsible with a title. If a person does not display the values of the organization prior to a promotion, it is doubtful he will display the values of the organization after a promotion.

Team members with aspirations of leadership must not wait for titles and positions to lead—lead now through serving. Paul Chappell, in *Leaders Who Make a Difference,* says, "There is no preparation for ministry like finding a place to serve in the battle and staying in it! Don't wait until the 'big opportunity' comes your way; simply look for an opportunity to serve where you are."[208]

Model Servanthood

How will others know what serving is? What it looks like? What it entails? They will know by watching what you do. The reason some refrain from serving is simply because they are emulating leadership. If you want others to serve, start serving others.

Leaders must do more than talk about serving; leaders must model serving by serving those they are calling on to serve. This is what Jesus did. He led by example. "At the last supper,

Jesus modeled servanthood by washing His disciples' feet—including Judas Iscariot, the one who would betray Him!"[209] Some leaders think serving is beneath them. Jesus, however, showed us secure leaders serve.

> Jesus knew His position and was willing not to flaunt it. He knew His calling and was willing to be faithful to it. He knew His future and was willing to submit to it. He had nothing to prove, nothing to lose, and nothing to hide. He was into towels not titles.[210]

Throughout Scripture we see those who serve were empowered to lead—Paul, Stephen, Philip, and others.

Paul, an incredible leader, refers to himself as a servant more so than as an apostle, teacher, or any other role. Paul also describes several of his fellow workers as servants—Phoebe, Apollos, Timothy, and Tychicus. Furthermore, "In his most extended reflection on the matter Paul describes himself and Apollos as 'only servants' and emphasizes their unimportance and lowly status in contrast to how the Corinthians speak of themselves (1 Cor. 3:5-4:13)."[211]

What is a servant? What is servant-leadership? What does it entail? Some think servants take care of the mundane matters and menial tasks, while leaders are responsible for the more important matters. But in all actuality, serving is about "the way any task is undertaken rather than what task is being undertaken."[212] When it comes to servant-leaders, Tom Marshall, in *Understand Leadership*, explains, "The first thing we have to get clear is that we are dealing with a question of character or nature, not a question of function."[213] This is not to say that leaders do not function as servants. Clearly, Christ died on the cross. However, what He did flowed from who He was.

What about you? Would you describe yourself as a servant first, leader second? Are you willing to live the life of a servant? If so, like Christ, you will serve those you are calling on to serve. This means you will:[214]

- Always seek the best interests of those you lead.

- Always find satisfaction in the progress of those you lead.

- Willingly accept the obligations of leadership.

- Have a desire to be accountable.

- Express caring love for those you lead.

- Be willing to listen.

It's Okay to Be a Servant

Some people have wrong ideas about leadership. When they get a position or title, it changes the way they act towardpeople. The problem, however, is not the position or title. Positions and titles do not change people; they just reveal people for who they really are.

Unfortunately, many leaders have fallen after having achieved success. Successful people must be careful not to surround themselves with people who will stroke their egos and tell them what they want to hear; they must be careful not to surround themselves with "yes" people.

Success does not give a person the right to be rude or disrespectful to others. Likewise, while those who obtain success should not look down on the "have nots," it is equally wrong for those who "have not" to resent those who do.

Proverbs 16:18 says, "Pride goes before destruction, and a haughty spirit before a fall." A person can be prideful and never hold a position or title or achieve success. Pride is a matter of the heart, not positions or possessions. Neither positions nor possessions make a man; they simply reveal a man.

Some people think humility is a sign of weakness. But humility is not a sign of weakness; humility is a sign of strength. People with humility do not have a need to impress others. They are content with who they are, where they are, and where they are headed. People with humility are comfortable being who they are.

Are you a prideful person or a humble person? Do you know the difference between the two? Humble leaders are givers; prideful leaders are takers. Humble leaders listen; prideful leaders want everyone else to do the listening. Humble leaders share the credit; prideful leaders hoard the credit. Humble leaders always are willing to learn; prideful leaders think they already know it all. Humble leaders empower others; prideful leaders hold on to power.

One of the greatest things a man could ever do is to pursue humility. Paul writes in Philippians 2:3-4,

> Let nothing be done through selfish ambition or conceit, but in lowliness of mind let each esteem others better than himself. Let each of you look out not only for his own interests, but also for the interests of others.

He continues in verses 7-11, describing the path of humility:

> But made Himself (Jesus) of no reputation, taking the form of a bondservant, and coming in the likeness of men. And being found in appearance as a man, He humbled Himself and became obedient to the point of death, even the death of the cross. Therefore God also has highly exalted Him and given Him the name which is above every name, that at the name of Jesus every knee should bow, of those in heaven, and of those on earth, and of those under the earth, and that every tongue should confess that Jesus Christ is Lord, to the glory of God the Father.

God always exalts the humble. Always has; always will. Pride will bring a man low, but humility will prepare him for honor.[215]

Conclusion

When teams are empowered, extraordinary things can occur. But for this to happen all parties involved—leaders and team members—must serve and do so with humility. Through empowerment, becoming servants, and retaining humility, succession issues can be done away with. There is a better way; it is through empowerment. Everyone needs an empowered team.

EPILOGUE

Bruce Tuckman's model for group development explains how teams evolve through various phases of growth and how leaders change leadership style, or focus, to help teams transition successfully from one stage to another. When Tuckman first introduced his model, it consisted of four stages: forming, storming, norming, and performing. He later added a fifth stage—adjourning.[216]

Adjourning is described as the phase in which a group breaks up, hopefully after it has successfully completed its task. From an organizational perspective, successful adjourning involves sensitivity and recognition of people's feelings as people move on to other projects and other things. Unfortunately, in many situations team members are uncertain as to whether or not their efforts and time were appreciated.

Leaders can help team members adjourn. They can do this by giving honor to whom honor is due; by helping team members transition to new roles and responsibilities; by continuing to help team members align with their gifts as their gifts continue to mature; by validating God's call on people's lives; and perhaps most importantly, by releasing and supporting people who move on to other things in other places. Leaders who participate in adjourning are Kingdom leaders. They understand the big picture extends beyond their immediate surroundings. This is the type of leader all church leaders should be.

But not only is adjourning a leader's responsibility, it is also the responsibility of team members, especially when the team has successfully moved from one stage to another and accomplished its purpose. Team members, of all people, should celebrate and support each other's successes. After all, what a person has become is a result of what a person has endured, usually with others

The focus of this book has been teams. We have addressed the need for teams; importance of teams; how to build, grow, and work with teams; and what the empowerment of teams entails. My hope is that you have gained some insight that will help you in developing and building successful teams.

Finally, it is my sincere prayer that you feel encouraged to build a team. You can do it. The power resides in you and those you lead. God placed it there. I believe the success of your ministry and leadership, as well as the organization you lead, is dependent upon it.

BIBLIOGRAPHY

"Coral," *Tuckman's Stages of Group Development.* Accessed April 3, 2014. http://coral.wcupa.edu/tuckman.htm.

Argyris, Chris. "Initiating Change that Preserves," *Journal of Public Administration Research and Theory* 3 (1994): 343-355.

Arnold, Josh A., Sharon Arad, Jonathan A. Rhoades, and Fritz Drasgow. "The Empowering Leadership Questionnaire: The Construction and Validation of a New Scale for Measuring Leader Behaviors," *Journal of Organizational Behavior* 21 (2000): 249–269.

Barna Group, "Prodigal Pastor Kids: Fact or Fiction." *Barna Group.* November 12, 2013. https://www.barna.org/barna-update/family-kids/644-prodigal-pastor-kids-fact-or-fiction#.Uv1fTEJdWi0.

Barna, George. *The Power of Team Leadership: Achieving Success through Shared Responsibility.* Colorado Springs, CO: WaterBrook Press, 2001.

Barzun, Jacques. *From Dawn to Decadence.* New York: HarperCollins, 2000.

Blackaby, Henry and Richard Blackaby. *Spiritual Leadership: Moving People on to God's Agenda.* Nashville, TN: Broadman & Holman Publishers, 2001.

Blanchard, Ken, John Carlos, and Alan Randolph. *Empowerment Takes More Than a Minute*. San Francisco, CA: Berrett-Koehler Publishers, 1996.

Bose, Partha. *Alexander the Great's Art of Strategy: Lessons from the Great Empire Builder*. New York: Penguin Group, 2003.

Burkus, David. *The Myths of Creativity: The Truth About How Innovative Companies and People Generate Great Ideas*. San Francisco, CA: Jossey-Bass, 2014.

Business Dictionary. "Team," accessed February 3, 2014, http://www.businessdictionary.com/definition/team.html#ixzz2rnjnxudG.

Carlock, Randel S. "Assessment Tools for Developing and Leading Effective Teams." Working paper. Entrepreneurship and Family Enterprise. Insead, Singapore. 2012. http://www.insead.edu/facultyresearch/research/doc.cfm?did=49811.

Chaleff, Ira. *The Courageous Follower: Standing Up to & For Our Leaders* 2nd ed. San Francisco, CA: Berrett-Koehler Publishers, 2003.

Chappell, Paul. *Leaders Who Make a Difference: Leadership Lessons from Three Great Bible Leaders*. Lancaster, CA: Striving Together Publications, 2009, Kindle Edition.

Conley, Randy. "Four Words a Boss Never Wants to Hear." *Blanchard LeaderChat*. June 27, 2013. http://leaderchat.org/2013/06/27/four-words-a-boss-never-wants-to-hear/.

Constable, Thomas. "Expository Notes of Dr. Thomas Constable." *StudyLight.org.* Accessed April 4, 2014. http://www.studylight.org/commentaries/dcc/view.cgi?bk=41&ch=6#bibliography.

Cotton, Sarah, Maureen Dollard, Jan de Jonge, and Paul Whetham. *"Clergy in Crisis," Occupational Stress in the Service Profession* Eds. Maureen Dollard, Anthony Winefield and Helen Winefield. London: Taylor & Francis, 2003: 311-358.

Covey, Stephen. *The 7 Habits of Highly Effective People.* Carlsbad, CA: Hay House, 2003.

Croce, Pat. *I Feel Great and You Will Too!* New York: Touchstone, 2001.

Dolan, Shimon L. and Salvador Garcia. "Managing by Values: Cultural Redesign for Strategic Organizational Change at the Dawn of the Twenty-First Century," *Journal of Management Development* 21 no. 2 (2001): 101-117.

Easum, Bill and Bill Tenny-Brittian. "Make Leaders or Make Disciples? Yes!" *Net Results Magazine.* November-December, 2012. Accessed April 15, 2014. http://netresults.org/wp-content/uploads/2013/04/2012-11-16.pdf.

Edmondson, Ron. "7 Signs You Might Be a Controlling Leader." *Ron Edmondson.* Accessed February 3, 2014. http://www.ronedmondson.com/2011/01/7-warning-signs-you-may-be-a-controlling-leader.html.

Ehrensperger, Kathy. *Paul and the Dynamics of Power: Communication and Interaction in the Early Christ-Movement.* London: T & T Clark, 2007.

Ellis, Joseph J. *Founding Brother: The Revolutionary Generation.* New York: Alfred A. Knope, 2000.

Elmore, Tim. "The Top Ten Leadership Principles of Jesus." *Growing Leaders.* Accessed on May 9, 2014. http://www.growouragleaders.com/PPTsandDOCs/leadership%20articles/Jesus%20Principles.doc.

Ephesians 4:12-13 Commentary. "Ephesians 4:12-13 Commentary." Accessed July 9, 2012. http://preceptaustin.org/ephesians_412-13.htm.

Fowler, Susan. "If You Are Holding People Accountable, Something Is Wrong." *Blanchard LeaderChat.* October 7, 2013. http://leaderchat.org/2013/10/07/if-you-are-holding-people-accountable-scmething-is-wrong-and-it-isnt-what-you-think/.

Gill, John. "John Gill's Exposition of the Bible," *Bible Study Tools.* Accessed March 25, 2014. http://www.biblestudytools.com/commentaries/gills-exposition-of-the-bible/luke-6-12.html.

Goldsmith, Marshall. *What Got You Here Won't Get You There.* New York: Hyperion, 2007.

Goldsworthy, Graeme. *Gospel and Kingdom: A Christian Interpretation of the Old Testament*, United Kingdom: Paternoster Press, 1981.

Grudem, Wayne. *Systematic Theology*. Grand Rapids, MI: Zondervan, 1994.

Hargrove, D. G. "Breaking the Barriers." *Apostolic Leaders Network*. Accessed February 22, 2014. http://aleaders.org/2013/02/01/breaking-the-barriers/.

Hartford Institute for Religion Research, "Fast Facts about American Religion." Accessed February 4, 2014. http://hirr.hartsem.edu/research/fastfacts/fast_facts.html.

Hawkins, Greg L. and Cally Parkinson. *Reveal Where Are You?* South Barrington, IL: Willow Creek Resources, 2007.

Hoekema, Anthony A. *The Bible and the Future*. Cumbria, CA: Eerdmans, 1979.

Hofstede, Geert. "National Culture: Countries." *Geert Hofstede*. Accessed July 12, 2012. http://geert-hofstede.com/united-states.html.

Ingram, Larry C. "Notes on Pastoral Power in the Congregational Tradition," *Journal for the Scientific Study of Religion* 19 no. 1 (1980): 40-48.

Iverson, Dick with Ray Grant. *Team Ministry: Putting Together a Team That Makes Churches Grow.* Portland, Oregon: City Bible Publishing, 1984.

Katzenbach, Jon R. and Douglas K. Smith. *The Wisdom of Teams: Creating the High-Performance Organization*. Boston, MA: Harvard Business School, 1993.

Kouzes, James M. and Barry Z. Posner. *Credibility: How Leaders Gain and Lose It, Why People Demand It*. San Francisco, CA: Jossey-Bass, 2003.

Krejcir, Richard J. "Statistics on Pastors." *Into Thy Word*. Accessed January 20, 2014. http://www.intothyword.org/apps/articles/?articleid=36562.

Ladd, George Eldon. *The Gospel of the Kingdom*. Grand Rapids, MI: Wm. B. Eerdmans, 1959.

London Jr., H. B. *Pastors at Greater Risk*. Ventura, CA: Regal Books, 2003.

Lowry, Lindy. "3 Movement-Making Shifts to Help Your Church Win." *Church Plants*. Accessed February 10, 2014. http://www.churchplants.com/how-tos/5752-3-movement-making-shifts-to-help-your-church-win.html.

Luther, Martin. *Brainy Quote*. Accessed February 12, 2014. http://www.brainyquote.com/quotes/quotes/m/martinluth390009.html.

MacMillian, Pat. The Performance Factor: Unlocking the Secrets of Teamwork, Nashville: TN, B&H Publishing Group, 2001.

Malphurs, Aubrey and Will Mancini. *Building Leaders: Blueprints for Developing Leaders at Every Level of Your Church*. Grand Rapids, MI: Baker Books, 2004.

Malphurs, Aubrey. "Leadership Development Insights From Ephesians 4." *Catalyst*. Accessed February 4, 2014.

http://catalystconference.com/read/leadership-development-insight-from-ephesians-4.

Malphurs, Aubrey. *Advanced Strategic Planning: A New Model for Church and Ministry Leaders.* Grand Rapids, Michigan: Baker Books, 2006.

Mancheno-Smoak, Lolita, Grace M. Endres and Yvonne A. Athanasaw. "The Individual Cultural Values and Job Satisfaction of the Transformational Leader," *Organizational Development Journal* 27 no. 3 (2009): 9-21.

Manktelow, James. "Forming, Storming, Norming, and Performing: Understanding the Stages of Team Formation." *Mind Tools.* Accessed April 10, 2014. http://www.mindtools.com/pages/article/newLDR_86.htm.

Maranatha's Life. "Statistics About Pastors." *Maranatha's Life Life-Line For Pastors.* Accessed June 30, 2012. http://maranathalife.com/lifeline/stats.htm

Marshall, Tom. *Understanding Leadership* Grand Rapids, MI: Baker Books, 2003.

Maslach, Christina and Michael P Leiter. *Handbook of Stress Medicine and Health* ed. London: CRC Press, 2005.

Merriam-Webster Dictionary Online. "Empowerment," accessed May 15, 2014, http://www.merriam-webster.com/dictionary/empower.

Merriam-Webster Dictionary. "Burnout," accessed January 23, 2014, http://www.merriam-webster.com/dictionary/burnout.

Merriam-Webster Dictionary. "Philosophy," accessed February 8, 2014, http://www.merriam-webster.com/dictionary/philosophy.

Merriam-Webster Dictionary. "Synergy," accessed February 3, 2014, http://www.merriam-webster.com/dictionary/synergy.

Merriam-Webster Dictionary. "Team," accessed January 31, 2014, http://www.merriam-webster.com/dictionary/team.

Mintzberg, Henry, Bruce Ahlstrand, and Joseph Lampel. *Strategy Safari: A Guided Tour Through the Wilds of Strategic Management.* New York: The Free Press, 2005.

Morgan, Tony. *Developing a Theology of Leadership,* 2012, Kindle Edition.

Nagel, Norman. "The Twelve and the Seven in Acts 6 and the Needy," *Concordia* (2005): 113-126.

Namie, Gary and Ruth Namie. *The Bully at Work: What You Can Do to Stop the Hurt and Reclaim Your Dignity on the Job.* Naperville, IL: Sourcebooks, 2000.

Nelson, Alan. "From Me to We." Accessed July 3, 2012. http://www.rev.org/article.asp?ID=2729.

Nieuwhof, Carey. "Why We Need More Entrepreneurial Church Leaders, Not More Shepherds." *CareyNieuwhof.com.* March 24, 2014. http://careynieuwhof.com/2014/03/why-we-need-more-entrepreneurial-church-leaders-not-more-shepherds/#sthash.MO99Yn3K.dpuf.

Northouse, Peter G. *Leadership: Theory and Practice* 4th ed. Thousand Oaks: Sage Publications, 2007.

Oxford Dictionaries. "Value," accessed February 20, 2014, http://www.oxforddictionaries.com/definition/english/value.

Parker, Glen M. *Team Players and Teamwork: The New Competitive Business Strategy.* San Francisco, CA: Jossey-Bass.

Pastor, Paul. "No More One-Man Band." *Christianity Today.* March 2014. Accessed April 13, 2014. http://www.christianitytoday.com/le/2014/march/no-more-one-man-band.html.

Prestwood, Donna C.L. and Paul A. Schumann Jr. "Seven New Principles of Leadership." *Futurist* 31, no. 1 (1997): 68.

Proeschold-Bell, Rae Jean and Sara LeGrand. "High Rates of Obesity and Chronic Disease among United Methodist Clergy." *Obesity* 18 no. 9 (n.d.): 1867-1870.

Rainer, Thom S. "7 Traits of Breakout Churches." *Outreach Magazine.* Accessed February 11, 2014. http://www.outreachmagazine.com/features/4817-7-traits-of-breakout-churches.html.

Rainer, Thom S. "Four Reasons Most Churches Aren't Breakout Churches." *Thom S. Rainer.* April 20, 2013. http://thomrainer.com/2013/04/20/four-simple-reasons-most-churches-arent-breakout-churches/.

Rainer, Thom S. "How Many Hours Must a Pastor Work to Satisfy the Congregation?" *Thom Rainer.* July 24, 2013.

http://thomrainer.com/2013/07/24/how-many-hours-must-a-pastor-work-to-satisfy-the-congregation/.

Rainer, Thom S. "Seven Occasions When You Should Not Hire More Church Staff." *Thom S. Rainer.* February 22, 2014. http://thomrainer.com/2014/02/22/seven-occasions-when-you-should-not-hire-more-church-staff/.

Rainer, Thom S. *Breakout Churches: Discover How to Make the Leap.* Grand Rapids, MI: Zondervan, 2005.

Robert, Mark D. "What is the Kingdom of God." *Patheos.* May 6, 2011. http://www.patheos.com/blogs/markdroberts/2011/05/06/what-is-the-kingdom-of-god/.

Scaramanga, Url. "Pastors are Fatter, Sicker, & more Depressed." August 6, 2010. http://www.christianitytoday.com/parse/.

Scaramanga, Url. "Willow Creek Repents? Why the Most Influential Church in America Now Says 'We Made a Mistake.'" *Leadership Journal.* October 18, 2007. http://outofur.com/archives/2007/10/willow_creek_re.html.

Schobert, Steve. "Pastoral Leadership: It Takes a Team." Unpublished manuscript. Urshan Graduate School of Theology. Florissant, MO, 2013.

Sell, Phillip W. "The Seven in Acts 6 as a Ministry Team," *Bibliotheca Sacra* 167, no. 665 (2010): 58-67.

Sloane, Matt, Jason Hanna and Dana Ford. "'Never, Ever Give Up' Diana Nyad Completes Historic Cuba-to-Florida Swim." *CNN World.* September 3, 2013. http://www.

cnn.com/2013/09/02/world/americas/diana-nyad-cuba-florida-swim/.

Sokoll, Shane M. "Are You an Empowered, Empowering Leader." *Enrichment Journal.* 2014. Accessed May 11, 2014. http://enrichmentjournal.ag.org/201203/201203_EJO_empowered_leader.cfm.

Strongs. "Shepherd." *Blue Letter Bible.* Accessed February 11, 2014. http://www.blueletterbible.org/lang/lexicon/lexicon.cfm?Strongs=G4166.

Sutton, Robert and Hayagreeva Rao. *Scaling Up Excellence.* New York: Crown Business, 2014.

Svoboda, Matt. "The Dangers of Entrepreneurship in Pastoral Ministry." *Matt Svoboda.* February 13, 2014. http://mattsvo.com/2014/02/13/the-dangers-of-entrepreneurship-killing-pastoral-ministry-in-pastoral-ministry/.

Thacther, Margaret. *Brainy Quote.* Accessed May 2, 2014. http://www.brainyquote.com/quotes/quotes/m/margaretth109592.html.

Tidball, Derek. "Leaders as Servants: A Resolution of the Tension," *Evangelical Review of Theology* 36, no. 1 (2012): 31-47.

Tuckman, Bruce and Mary Ann C. Jensen. "Stages of Small Group Development Revisited," *Group and Organizational Studies* 2 (1977): 419-427.

Tuckman, Bruce. "Developmental Sequence in Small Groups." *Psychological Bulletin* 63 (1965): 384-399.

Van der Heyden, Ludo, Christine Blondel, and Randel S. Carlock. "Fair Process: Striving for Justice in Family Business," *Family Business Review* 18, no. 1 (2005): 1-21.

Viola, Frank and George Barna. *Pagan Christianity: Exploring the Roots of Our Church Practices*. Tyndale, 2012.

Vitello, Paul. "Taking a Break From the Lord's Work." *The New York Times*. August 1, 2010. http://www.nytimes.com/2010/08/02/nyregion/02burnout.html?pagewanted=all.

Warren, Rick. "3 Fears That Prevent Leaders from Being Authentic and Influencing People." *Pastors.com*. Accessed January 9, 2014. http://pastors.com/fears-authenticity/.

Weaver, Andrew J., David B. Larson, Kevin J. Flannelly, Harold G. Koenig, and Carolyn L. Stapleton. "Mental Health Issues Among Clergy and Other Religious Professionals: A Review of Research," *The Journal of Pastoral Care & Counseling* 56, no. 4 (2002): 393-403.

Wheeler, Raiford S. *A View from the Parsonage*. Xulon Press, 2012.

Wilson, Eugene T. *Realign: God-Called Leaders and Connecting with Their Purpose*, Hazelwood, MO: Word Aflame Press, 2013.

Zigarmi, Drea. "Just Leadership: Creating a Value-Driven Community," *Executive Forum* (2008): 33-38.

ENDNOTES

CHAPTER ONE: **A CRY FOR HELP**
[1] George Barna, *The Power of Team Leadership: Achieving Success through Shared Responsibility* (Colorado Springs, CO: WaterBrook Press, 2001), 1.
[2] Ibid, 2-3.
[3] Ibid, 3.
[4] Ibid, 3-4.
[5] Ibid, 4.
[6] Dick Iverson with Ray Grant, *Team Ministry: Putting Together a Team That Makes Churches Grow* (Portland, Oregon: City Bible Publishing, 1984), 8.
[7] Andrew J. Weaver, et.al., "Mental Health Issues Among Clergy and Other Religious Professionals: A Review of Research," *The Journal of Pastoral Care & Counseling* 56.4 (2002) 395.
[8] Maranatha's Life, "Statistics About Pastors," *Maranatha's Life Life-Line For Pastors,* accessed June 30, 2012, http://maranathalife.com/lifeline/stats.html.
[9] Sarah Cotton, et.al., *"Clergy in Crisis," Occupational Stress in the Service Profession* Eds. Maureen Dollard, Anthony Winefield and Helen Winefield, (London: Taylor & Francis, 2003), 311-358.
[10] Thom S. Rainer, "How Many Hours Must a Pastor Work to Satisfy the Congregation?" *Thom Rainer,* July 24, 2013 http://thomrainer.com/2013/07/24/how-many-hours-must-a-pastor-work-to-satisfy-the-congregation/.
[11] Ibid.
[12] Steve Schobert, "Pastoral Leadership: It Takes a Team," (Unpublished manuscript, Urshan Graduate School of Theology, Florissant, MO, 2013).
[13] Paul Vitello, "Taking a Break From the Lord's Work."

The New York Times, August 1, 2010, http://www.nytimes.com/2010/08/02/nyregion/02burnout.html?pagewanted=all.

[14] Rae Jean Proeschold-Bell and Sara LeGrand, "High Rates of Obesity and Chronic Disease among United Methodist Clergy," *Obesity* 18 (n.d.): 9, 1867-1870. http://divinity.duke.edu/sites/default/files/documents/chi/High%20rates%20of%20obesity%20and%20chronic%20disease%20among%20UMC%20clergy_formatted.pdf.

[15] Vitello, "Taking a Break From the Lord's Work."

[16] H. B. London Jr., *Pastors at Greater Risk* (Ventura, CA: Regal Books, 2003).

[17] Maranatha's Life, "Statistics About Pastors."

[18] Weaver, "Mental Health Issues Among Clergy and Other Religious Professionals."

[19] Ibid.

[20] Url Scaramanga, "Pastors are Fatter, Sicker, & more Depressed," August 6, 2010, http://www.christianitytoday.com/parse/.

[21] Barna Group, "Prodigal Pastor Kids: Fact or Fiction," *Barna Group,* November 12, 2013, https://www.barna.org/barna-update/family-kids/644-prodigal-pastor-kids-fact-or-fiction#.Uv1fTEJdWi0.

[22] London Jr., *Pastors at Greater Risk.*

[23] Raiford S. Wheeler, *A View from the Parsonage* (Xulon Press, 2012).

[24] London Jr., *Pastors at Greater Risk.*

[25] Maranatha's Life, "Statistics About Pastors."

[26] Ibid.

[27] *Merriam-Webster Dictionary,* "Burnout," accessed January 23, 2014, http://www.merriam-webster.com/dictionary/burnout.

[28] Christina Maslach and Michael P Leiter, "Stress and Burnout: The Critical Research," *Handbook of Stress Medicine and Health* ed. Cary Cooper, (London: CRC Press, 2005).

[29] Frank Viola and George Barna. *Pagan Christianity:*

Exploring the Roots of Our Church Practices. (Tyndale, 2012).
   [30]Maranatha's Life, "Statistics About Pastors."
   [31]Wheeler, *A View from the Parsonage*.
   [32]Richard J. Krejcir, "Statistics on Pastors," *Into Thy Word*, accessed January 20, 2014, http://www.intothyword.org/apps/articles/?articleid=36562.
   [33]Ibid.
   [34]Numbers 11:15
   [35]I Kings 19:4

CHAPTER TWO: **EVERYONE NEEDS A TEAM**
   [36]Mark 8:27-29
   [37]Luke 9:23-24
   [38]Numbers 11:16-17
   [39]I Kings 19:16
   [40]John 16:11
   [41]*Merriam-Webster Dictionary*, "Team," accessed on January 31, 2014, http://www.merriam-webster.com/dictionary/team.
   [42]*Business Dictionary*, "Team," accessed February 3, 2014, http://www.businessdictionary.com/definition/team.html#ixzz2rnjnxudG.
   [43]Jon R. Katzenbach and Douglas K. Smith, *The Wisdom of Teams: Creating the High-Performance Organization* (Boston, MA: Harvard Business School, 1993), 45.
   [44]Peter G. Northouse, *Leadership: Theory and Practice 4th ed* (Thousand Oaks: Sage Publications, 2007), 3.
   [45]Henry Blackaby and Richard Blackaby, *Spiritual Leadership: Moving People on to God's Agenda* (Nashville, TN: Bradman & Holman Publishers, 2001).
   [46]Northouse, *Leadership: Theory and Practice 4th ed*.
   [47]Geert Hofstede, "National Culture: Countries," *Geert Hofstede*, accessed July 12, 2012, http://geert-hofstede.com/united-states.html.
   [48]Steve Schobert, "Pastoral Leadership: It Takes a Team,"

(Unpublished manuscript, Urshan Graduate School of Theology, Florissant, MO, 2013).

[49] Ibid.

[50] Wayne Grudem, *Systematic Theology* (Grand Rapids, MI: Zondervan, 1994), 859.

[51] Aubrey Malphurs, *Advanced Strategic Planning: A New Model for Church and Ministry Leaders* (Grand Rapids, Michigan: Baker Books, 2006), 212.

[52] *Merriam-Webster Dictionary,* "Synergy," accessed February 3, 2014, http://www.merriam-webster.com/dictionary/synergy.

[53] *Business Dictionary*, "Team."

[54] Pat Croce, *I Feel Great and You Will Too!* (New York: Touchstone, 2001), 159.

[55] Ibid, 59.

[56] Phillip W. Sell, "The Seven in Acts 6 as a Ministry Team," *Bibliotheca Sacra* 167 (2010): 665, 59.

[57] Norman Nagel, "The Twelve and the Seven in Acts 6 and the Needy," *Concordia*, (2005): 113-126.

[58] Ibid, 117.

[59] Ibid, 117.

[60] Sell, "The Seven in Acts 6 as a Ministry Team."

[61] Thom S. Rainer, *Breakout Churches: Discover How to Make the Leap* (Grand Rapids, MI: Zondervan, 2005).

[62] Thom S. Rainer, "7 Traits of Breakout Churches," *Outreach Magazine*, accessed February 11, 2014, http://www.outreachmagazine.com/features/4817-7-traits-of-breakout-churches.html.

[63] Hartford Institute for Religion Research, "Fast Facts About American Religion," accessed February 4, 2014, http://hirr.hartsem.edu/research/fastfacts/fast_facts.html.

[64] Ibid.

[65] Ibid.

[66] Ibid.

[67] Larry C. Ingram, "Notes on Pastoral Power in the Congregational Tradition," *Journal for the Scientific Study of Religion* 19 (1980): 1, 40-48.

[68] Strongs, "Shepherd," *Blue Letter Bible,* accessed February 11, 2014, http://www.blueletterbible.org/lang/lexicon/lexicon.cfm?Strongs=G4166.

[69] Alan Nelson, "From Me to We," accessed July 3, 2012, http://www.rev.org/article.asp?ID=2729 (para. 2).

[70] Ibid.

[71] George Barna, *The Power of Team Leadership: Achieving Success through Shared Responsibility.* (Colorado Springs, CO: WaterBrook Press, 2001), 8.

[72] Steve Schobert, "Pastoral Leadership: It Takes a Team."

[73] Thom S. Rainer, "Four Reasons Most Churches Aren't Breakout Churches," *Thom S. Rainer,* April 20, 2013, http://thomrainer.com/2013/04/20/four-simple-reasons-most-churches-arent-breakout-churches/.

CHAPTER THREE: **NEW PARADIGMS, OLD PURPOSE**

[74] Aubrey Malphurs and Will Mancini, *Building Leaders: Blueprints for Developing Leaders at Every Level of Your Church,* (Grand Rapids, MI: Baker Books, 2004), 2.

[75] Eugene T. Wilson, *Realign: God-Called Leaders and Connecting with Their Purpose* (Hazelwood, MO: Word Aflame Press, 2013).

[76] *Ephesians 4:12-13 Commentary*, "Ephesians 4:12-13 Commentary," accessed July 9, 2012, http://preceptaustin.org/ephesians_412-13.htm.

[77] Alan Nelson, "From Me to We," accessed July 3, 2012, http://www.rev.org/article.asp?ID=2729.

[78] Aubrey Malphurs, "Leadership Development Insights From Ephesians 4," *Catalyst* accessed February 4, 2014, http://catalystconference.com/read/leadership-development-insight-from-ephesians-4.

[79] Ibid.

CHAPTER FOUR: **PHILOSOPHIES, PRINCIPLES, AND A KING**

[80]*Merriam-Webster Dictionary.* "Philosophy," accessed February 8, 2014, http://www.merriam-webster.com/dictionary/philosophy.

[81]D. G. Hargrove, "Breaking the Barriers," *Apostolic Leaders Network,* accessed February 22, 2014, http://aleaders.org/2013/02/01/breaking-the-barriers/.

[82]Matthew 6:19-20

[83]Martin Luther, *Brainy Quote,* accessed February 12, 2014, http://www.brainyquote.com/quotes/quotes/m/martinluth390009.html.

[84]Matt Sloane, et.al., "'Never, Ever Give Up' Diana Nyad Completes Historic Cuba-to-Florida Swim," *CNN World,* September 3, 2013, http://www.cnn.com/2013/09/02/world/americas/diana-nyad-cuba-florida-swim/.

[85]Ron Edmondson, "7 Signs You Might Be a Controlling Leader," *Ron Edmondson* accessed February 3, 2014, http://www.ronedmondson.com/2011/01/7-warning-signs-you-may-be-a-controlling-leader.html.

[86]Donna C.L. Prestwood and Paul A. Schumann Jr., "Seven New Principles of Leadership," *Futurist* 31 (1997): 1, 68.

[87]Ibid, 68.
[88]Ibid, 68.
[89]Ibid, 68.
[90]Ibid, 68.
[91]Ibid, 68.
[92]Ibid, 68.
[93]Ibid, 68.

[94]Lindy Lowry, "3 Movement-Making Shifts to Help Your Church Win," Church Plants accessed February 10, 2014, http://www.churchplants.com/how-tos/5752-3-movement-making-shifts-to-help-your-church-win.html.

[95]George Eldon Ladd, *The Gospel of the Kingdom* (Grand Rapids, MI: Wm. B. Eerdmans, 1959), 13-23. http://www.

gospelpedlar.com/articles/Last%20Things/kogladd.html.
[96]Graeme Goldsworthy, *Gospel and Kingdom: A Christian Interpretation of the Old Testament*, (United Kingdom: Paternoster Press, 1981, 53.
[97]Anthony A. Hoekema, *The Bible and the Future*, (Cumbria, CA: Eerdmans, 1979). 45.
[98]Ladd, *The Gospel of the Kingdom*.
[99]Mark D. Robert, "What is the Kingdom of God," *Patheos,* May 6, 2011, http://www.patheos.com/blogs/markdroberts/2011/05/06/what-is-the-kingdom-of-god/.
[100]Ibid.

CHAPTER FIVE: **VALUE-DRIVEN LEADERSHIP**

[101]*Oxford Dictionaries*, "Value," accessed February 20, 2014, http://www.oxforddictionaries.com/definition/english/value.
[102]Eugene T. Wilson, *Realign: God-Called Leaders and Connecting with Their Purpose* (Hazelwood, MO: Word Aflame Press, 2013), 124.
[103]Donna C.L., et.al., "Seven New Principles of Leadership," *Futurist*, 31 (1997): 1, 68.
[104]James M. Kouzes and Barry Z. Posner, *Credibility: How Leaders Gain and Lose It, Why People Demand It* (San Francisco, CA: Jossey-Bass, 2003).
[105]Shimon L. Dolan and Salvador Garcia, "Managing by Values: Cultural Redesign for Strategic Organizational Change at the Dawn of the Twenty-First Century," *Journal of Management Development*, 21 (2001): 2, 101-117.
[106]Drea Zigarmi, "Just Leadership: Creating a Value-Driven Community," *Executive Forum*. (2008), 34. http://www.academia.edu/3431285/Just_leadership_Creating_a_values-driven_community.
[107]Ibid. 34.
[108]Acts 20:29
[109]Lolita Mancheno-Smoak, et.al., "The Individual Cultural

Values and Job Satisfaction of the Transformational Leader," *Organizational Development Journal*, 27 (2009): 3, 9-21.
[110]Zigarmi, "Just Leadership: Creating a Value-Driven Community," 35.
[111]Margaret Thacther, *Brainy Quote*, accessed May 2, 2014, http://www.brainyquote.com/quotes/quotes/m/margaretth109592.html.
[112]Zigarmi, "Just Leadership: Creating a Value-Driven Community," 35.
[113]Randy Conley, "Four Words a Boss Never Wants to Hear," *Blanchard LeaderChat*, June 27, 2013, http://leaderchat.org/2013/06/27/four-words-a-boss-never-wants-to-hear/.
[114]Rick Warren, "3 Fears That Prevent Leaders from Being Authentic and Influencing People," *Pastors.com*, accessed January 9, 2014, http://pastors.com/fears-authenticity/.
[115]Zigarmi, "Just Leadership: Creating a Value-Driven Community." 35.
[116]Ibid. 35.
[117]D. G. Hargrove, "Breaking the Barriers," *Apostolic Leaders Network*, accessed February 22, 2014, http://aleaders.org/2013/02/01/breaking-the-barriers/.
[118]Mark 14:34
[119]Warren, "3 Fears That Prevent Leaders from Being Authentic and Influencing People."
[120]Ibid.
[121]Ibid.
[122]Ibid.
[123]Ibid.
[124]Robert Sutton and Hayagreeva Rao, *Scaling Up Excellence* (New York: Crown Business, 2014).
[125]Chris Argyris, "Initiating Change that Preserves," *Journal of Public Administration Research and Theory* 3 (1994): 345.

CHAPTER SIX: BUILDING TEAMS

[126] Aubrey Malphurs and William F. Mancini, *Building Leaders: Blueprints for Developing Leadership at Every Level of Your Church*. (Grand Rapids, Michigan: Baker Books, 2004), 24.

[127] Ibid, 11.

[128] Luke 6:12-16

[129] John Gill, "John Gill's Exposition of the Bible," *Bible Study Tools* accessed March 25, 2014, http://www.biblestudytools.com/commentaries/gills-exposition-of-the-bible/luke-6-12.html.

[130] Ibid.

[131] Thomas Constable, "Expository Notes of Dr. Thomas Constable," *StudyLight.org* accessed April 4, 2014, http://www.studylight.org/commentaries/dcc/view.cgi?bk=41&ch=6#bibliography.

[132] Exodus 18:21

[133] Marshall Goldsmith, *What Got You Here Won't Get You There* (New York: Hyperion, 2007).

[134] Ira Chaleff, *The Courageous Follower: Standing Up to & For Our Leaders* 2nd ed. (San Francisco: CA, Berrett-Koehler Publishers, 2003).

[135] Henry Mintzberg, et.al., *Strategy Safari: A Guided Tour Through the Wilds of Strategic Management* (New York: The Free Press, 2005).

[136] David Burkus, *The Myths of Creativity: The Truth About How Innovative Companies and People Generate Great Ideas* (San Francisco, CA: Jossey-Bass, 2014).

[137] Ibid. 108.

[138] Url Scaramanga, "Willow Creek Repents? Why the Most Influential Church in America Now Says 'We Made a Mistake.'" *Leadership Journal* (October 18, 2007), accessed May 11, 2011, http:// outofur.com/archives/2007/10/willow_creek_re.html.

[139] Greg L. Hawkins and Cally Parkinson, *Reveal Where Are You?* (South Barrington, IL: Willow Creek Resources, 2007).

[140] Thom S. Rainer, "Seven Occasions When You Should

Not Hire More Church Staff," Thom S. Rainer, February 22, 2014, http://thomrainer.com/2014/02/22/seven-occasions-when-you-should-not-hire-more-church-staff/

CHAPTER SEVEN: DEVELOPING TEAMS

[141] Marshall Goldsmith, *What Got You Here Won't Get You There* (New York: Hyperion, 2007).

[142] Bill Easum and Bill Tenny-Brittian, "Make Leaders or Make Disciples? Yes!" *Net Results Magazine* (November-December, 2012), 18. accessed April 15, 2014. http://netresults.org/wp-content/uploads/2013/04/2012-11-16.pdf.

[143] Ibid. 16.

[144] Ibid. 16.

[145] Stephen Covey, *The 7 Habits of Highly Effective People* (Carlsbad, CA: Hay House, 2003).

[146] Ibid.

[147] Ibid.

[148] Exodus 32:17

[149] Exodus 32:18, KJV

[150] Exodus 33:11

[151] Bruce Tuckman, "Developmental Sequence in Small Groups," *Psychological Bulletin* 63 (1965): 384-399. The article was reprinted in *Group Facilitation: A Research and Applications Journal* 3 (2001) and is available as a Word document: http://dennislearningcenter.osu.edu/references/GROUP%20DEV%20ARTICLE.doc.

[152] Ibid.

[153] "Coral," *Tuckman's Stages of Group Development*, accessed April 3, 2014. http://coral.wcupa.edu/tuckman.htm.

[154] Ibid.

[155] James Manktelow, "Forming, Storming, Norming, and Performing: Understanding the Stages of Team Formation." Mind Tools, accessed April 10, 2014. http://www.mindtools.com/pages/article/newLDR_86.htm.

CHAPTER EIGHT: **WORKING WITH TEAMS**

[156] Paul Chappell, *Leaders Who Make a Difference: Leadership Lessons from Three Great Bible Leaders* (Lancaster, CA: Striving Together Publications, 2009), Kindle Edition. 49-50.

[157] Carey Nieuwhof, "Why We Need More Entrepreneurial Church Leaders, Not More Shepherds," *CareyNieuwhof.com,* March 24, 2014, http://careynieuwhof.com/2014/03/why-we-need-more-entrepreneurial-church-leaders-not-more-shepherds/#sthash.MO99Yn3K.dpuf.

[158] Matt Svoboda, "The Dangers of Entrepreneurship in Pastoral Ministry," *Matt Svoboda,* February 13, 2014, http://mattsvo.com/2014/02/13/the-dangers-of-entrepreneurship-killing-pastoral-ministry-in-pastoral-ministry/.

[159] Kathy Ehrensperger, *Paul and the Dynamics of Power: Communication and Interaction in the Early Christ-Movement* (London: T & T Clark, 2007), 118-119.

[160] Ibid, 118-119.

[161] Ibid, 118-119.

[162] Ibid, 118-119.

[163] Ibid, 118-119.

[164] Susan Fowler, "If You Are Holding People Accountable, Something Is Wrong," *Blanchard LeaderChat,* October 7, 2013, http://leaderchat.org/2013/10/07/if-you-are-holding-people-accountable-something-is-wrong-and-it-isnt-what-you-think/.

[165] Ibid.

[166] Ibid.

[167] Ludo Van der Heyden, et.al., "Fair Process: Striving for Justice in Family Business," *Family Business Review* 18 (2005): 1, 1-21.

[168] Susan Fowler, "If You Are Holding People Accountable, Something Is Wrong."

[169] Ibid.

[170] Ibid.

[171] Ibid.

[172] Ira Chaleff, *The Courageous Follower: Standing Up to & For Our Leaders* 2nd ed. (San Francisco: CA, Berrett-Koehler Publishers, 2003), 50.

[173] Randel S. Carlock, "Assessment Tools for Developing and Leading Effective Teams," (working paper, Entrepreneurship and Family Enterprise, Insead, Singapore, 2012), http://www.insead.edu/facultyresearch/research/doc.cfm?did=49811.

[174] Ibid.

[175] Pat MacMillian, The Performance Factor: Unlocking the Secrets of Teamwork (Nashville: TN, B&H Publishing Group, 2001), 35.

[176] Phillip W. Sell, "The Seven in Acts 6 as a Ministry Team," *Bibliotheca Sacra* 167 (2010): 665, 53-67.

[177] Carlock, "Assessment Tools for Developing and Leading Effective Teams."

[178] Glen M. Parker, *Team Players and Teamwork: The New Competitive Business Strategy* (San Francisco, CA: Jossey-Bass).

[179] Parker, *Team Players and Teamwork: The New Competitive Business Strategy*, 88.

[180] Carlock, "Assessment Tools for Developing and Leading Effective Teams."

[181] Ibid.

[182] Ibid.

[183] Gary Namie and Ruth Namie, *The Bully at Work: What You Can Do to Stop the Hurt and Reclaim Your Dignity on the Job* (Naperville, IL: Sourcebooks, 2000).

CHAPTER NINE: **EMPOWERING TEAMS**

[184] *Merriam-Webster Dictionary Online,* "Empowerment," accessed May 15, 2014, http://www.merriam-webster.com/dictionary/empower.

[185] Tony Morgan, *Developing a Theology of Leadership,* (2012), Kindle Edition, 88-89.

[186] Ibid, 98.

[187] Ibid, 77-79.
[188] Shane M. Sokoll, "Are You an Empowered, Empowering Leader," *Enrichment Journal* (2014), accessed May 11, 2014, http://enrichmentjournal.ag.org/201203/201203_EJO_empowered_leader.cfm.
[189] Ibid.
[190] Ken Blanchard, et.al., *Empowerment Takes More Than a Minute,* (San Francisco, CA: Berrett-Koehler Publishers, 1996).
[191] Luke 22:25-27
[192] Blanchard, *Empowerment Takes More Than a Minute.*
[193] Josh A. Arnold, et.al., "The Empowering Leadership Questionnaire: The Construction and Validation of a New Scale for Measuring Leader Behaviors," *Journal of Organizational Behavior* 21 (2000): 249–269.
[194] Randel S. Carlock, "Assessment Tools for Developing and Leading Effective Teams," (working paper, Entrepreneurship and Family Enterprise, Insead, Singapore, 2012), http://www.insead.edu/facultyresearch/research/doc.cfm?did=49811.
[195] Partha Bose, *Alexander the Great's Art of Strategy: Lessons from the Great Empire Builder* (New York: Penguin Group, 2003).
[196] Ibid, 248.
[197] Ibid, 246.
[198] Tim Elmore, "The Top Ten Leadership Principles of Jesus," *Growing Leaders*, accessed on May 9, 2014. http://www.growouragleaders.com/PPTsandDOCs/leadership%20articles/Jesus%20Principles.doc.
[199] Paul Pastor, "No More One-Man Band," *Christianity Today,* (March 2014), accessed April 13, 2014. http://www.christianitytoday.com/le/2014/march/no-more-one-man-band.html.
[200] Ibid.
[201] Ibid.
[202] Ibid.

[203] Ibid.
[204] Ibid.
[205] Ibid.
[206] Ibid.
[207] Paul Chappell, *Leaders Who Make a Difference: Leadership Lessons from Three Great Bible Leaders* (Lancaster, CA: Striving Together Publications, 2009), Kindle Edition, 14-15.
[208] Ibid, 14-15.
[209] Elmore, "The Top Ten Leadership Principles of Jesus."
[210] Ibid.
[211] Derek Tidball, "Leaders as Servants: A Resolution of the Tension," *Evangelical Review of Theology* 36 (2012): 1, 38.
[212] Ibid, 39.
[213] Tom Marshall, *Understanding Leadership* (Grand Rapids, MI: Baker Books, 2003), 71.
[214] Tidball, "Leaders as Servants," 39.
[215] Proverbs 29:23

EPILOGUE
[216] Bruce Tuckman and Mary Ann C. Jensen, "Stages of Small Group Development Revisited,' *Group and Organizational Studies* 2 (1977): 419-427.

Also from Dr. Eugene T. Wilson:

Realign
Dr. Eugene Wilson

Realign redefines success of church leaders as the degree to which we help others become what God wants them to be rather than by the size of the crowd. It calls church leaders to realign with purpose, namely, equipping others for their work of ministry. It deals with the following concepts:
- The stages of life cycle of a church
- How people change and what you can do to help them keep it
- Your expectations for followers
- How church structures enhance or inhibit growth
- How maintaining a safe place increases involvement

| 25179 | Paperback | **$13.99** |
| 25508 | eBook | **$9.99** |

pentecostalpublishing.com